T0248429

Courage, Clarity & Confidence

Courage, Clarity & Confidence

REDEFINE SUCCESS
AND THE WAY YOU WORK

GALA JACKSON

Executive Career and Leadership Development Coach

WILEY

Copyright © 2024 by John Wiley & Sons, Inc. All rights reserved.

Published by John Wiley & Sons, Inc., Hoboken, New Jersey.
Published simultaneously in Canada.

No part of this publication may be reproduced, stored in a retrieval system, or transmitted in any form or by any means, electronic, mechanical, photocopying, recording, scanning, or otherwise, except as permitted under Section 107 or 108 of the 1976 United States Copyright Act, without either the prior written permission of the Publisher, or authorization through payment of the appropriate per-copy fee to the Copyright Clearance Center, Inc., 222 Rosewood Drive, Danvers, MA 01923, (978) 750-8400, fax (978) 750-4470, or on the web at www.copyright.com. Requests to the Publisher for permission should be addressed to the Permissions Department, John Wiley & Sons, Inc., 111 River Street, Hoboken, NJ 07030, (201) 748-6011, fax (201) 748-6008, or online at http://www.wiley.com/go/permission.

Limit of Liability/Disclaimer of Warranty: While the publisher and author have used their best efforts in preparing this book, they make no representations or warranties with respect to the accuracy or completeness of the contents of this book and specifically disclaim any implied warranties of merchantability or fitness for a particular purpose. No warranty may be created or extended by sales representatives or written sales materials. The advice and strategies contained herein may not be suitable for your situation. You should consult with a professional where appropriate. Further, readers should be aware that websites listed in this work may have changed or disappeared between when this work was written and when it is read. Neither the publisher nor authors shall be liable for any loss of profit or any other commercial damages, including but not limited to special, incidental, consequential, or other damages.

For general information on our other products and services or for technical support, please contact our Customer Care Department within the United States at (800) 762-2974, outside the United States at (317) 572-3993 or fax (317) 572-4002.

Wiley also publishes its books in a variety of electronic formats. Some content that appears in print may not be available in electronic formats. For more information about Wiley products, visit our web site at www.wiley.com.

Library of Congress Cataloging-in-Publication Data:

Names: Jackson, Gala, author.
Title: Courage, clarity, and confidence : redefining how successful women work / Gala Jackson.
Description: Hoboken, New Jersey : Wiley, [2024] | Includes index.
Identifiers: LCCN 2023043577 (print) | LCCN 2023043578 (ebook) | ISBN 9781119899402 (hardback) | ISBN 9781119899853 (adobe pdf) | ISBN 9781119899419 (epub)
Subjects: LCSH: Women—Employment. | Women—Vocational guidance. | Career development.
Classification: LCC HD6053 .J335 2024 (print) | LCC HD6053 (ebook) | DDC 331.4—dc23/eng/20231113
LC record available at https://lccn.loc.gov/2023043577
LC ebook record available at https://lccn.loc.gov/2023043578

Cover design: Paul McCarthy
Image credits: Courtesy of Marlyncia Pierce. MarMade Design Co.

SKY10062104_120823

*To my late father, Gregory, your love let me know I could be
and do anything*

*To my mom, Gloria, who taught me the strength of femininity
and always knew this book would be written*

*To my son, Grayson, your example of strength, determination,
and perseverance are the reason I finished this book – I love you
to the moon and back*

Contents

A Note from the Author

FROM THE TIME I opened an email from my editor inquiring about my interest in writing a book to the publication of that book, my life has done a complete 180. In the midst of writing this book, I had to redefine success for myself and it got real!

I went from being a single city girl to a married woman and bonus mom. I navigated a big move to a totally different community and culture just before my wedding. I had made my career the priority in my life for years, so I welcomed this new season in my personal life wholeheartedly.

In the midst of some of life's incredibly highest highs, I experienced the deepest of the lowest. I lost my father weeks prior to that email, and a few short months later my best friend – both unexpected. My father passed from a rare form of cancer just two weeks after his official diagnosis. My best friend died in a car accident, and when I got the call I found myself screaming in uncontrollable anguish, lying on my bedroom floor. In the midst of it all, I also had to put down my sweet dog of almost 18 years, she was my first baby. It all was unreal. It was all too much. It was traumatic.

I also experienced my first layoff from a company whose mission was personal – it wasn't just a job for me. The news came on my birthday while I was out on vacation. Yep, MY BIRTHDAY.

A week prior to the layoff announcement, I told my boss I was expecting my first child. I was completely shocked by the news and deeply worried about how the layoff was going to affect our family's financial plans.

And if those things weren't hard enough to navigate, I came to understand, in the most intimate way, the power of prayer and faith as I gave birth to my first child via emergency cesarean section before 30 weeks. A bouncing, healthy baby boy who came out breathing on his own, shocking the doctors with his strength and knocking his scores out of the park. After he spent a little over 9 weeks in the NICU, we got to take him home. He is a continuous reminder that miracles still happen every day. He changed my entire life. He unlocked the resilience and mental fortitude I would need to write this book.

The woman I was when I sat down to write this book evolved into a new woman I had not met before. I was equally intrigued and afraid of her in a reverential kind of way. Her strength and femininity were power on full display. My identity expanded and I submitted myself completely to the process and practice of growth. I am still growing.

I started and stopped writing this book more times than I can count. And I mean stopped writing completely. I was paralyzed by fear. I was uncertain of my voice and value. I didn't feel like an expert on anything, but rather a novice at everything.

How could I write about courage, clarity, or confidence when it seemed I had none of those things in that season? I honestly thought on more than one occasion, *I will never finish this book.* I experienced a full range of emotions in repetitive cycles. I was stripped down to my faith and foundation, which I scrutinized and turned inside out. Grief is unexplainable. So is love. Joy. Motherhood. And purpose. And writing.

The exact same principles I talk about in this book became a lamp to my feet as I reclaimed the essence of who I was and embodied the new woman I had become. I courageously observed, came into awareness, and explored with curiosity. Those observations, awareness, and exploration led me to locate and expand my values and reconnected me to my strengths. My experiences reminded me that I had survived 100% of my worst days and both the good and bad days were my teachers preparing me for the days to come.

Purpose and mission came into view again. Conviction gave way to confidence and there I realized I had something to say to women who, like me, were on the path to connecting with and embodying the strongest, boldest, most courageous version of themselves.

I found myself redefining success, work, and play again in light of how my life changed. Creating more room for something new, for freedom, abundance, and blessings. I learned we are truly on an evolutionary journey of becoming and I hope this book will be a trusted guide for you at every season in which you find yourself redefining – and *growing dynamically.*

As you read this book and step into my story, both personal and professional, I hope that you'll see yourself, accept the invitation to redefine success, and live out your authentic definition of success out loud so you too can experience what it's like to continuously live in the strongest, boldest, most courageous version of yourself.

May courage, confidence, and clarity be yours!

Introduction

I WROTE A book.

I always dreamed it could happen one day, but to actually be here at this moment writing to you is surreal, to say the least. I am writing the book I needed years ago, but I also recognize that in a lot of ways I am writing to who I am now too: still learning to embody my identity, values, vision, mission, and unapologetically be *me* in every room where I find myself. And I would be remiss if I did not acknowledge that I am writing to the women of the future, the women we collectively and individually aspire to be – I think that's my favorite part – finding connectivity between where I am today and the person I will be in a year or a few years from now. I believe, wholeheartedly, that no experience is ever wasted in life if you are a perpetual student of life. Every experience I have now will serve the woman I will be, and the same is true for you.

Every woman is on an evolutionary journey of becoming the woman she knows she can be. The woman who is far more than the opinions and expectations of others. The woman that we crave to be, one who is strong, bold, courageous, creative, and lives her truth. The woman who has been tucked inside of us all along, patiently waiting for us to introspectively discover how wise, beautiful, delicate, fierce, and powerful she really is. I firmly believe that our adult work is undoing all of the messaging we've been assigned as young women, returning to the true essence of who we are created to be on a soul level. The level where our heart and spirit is completely free to live the life that brings us peace, joy, safety, and comfort – the place where we can truly thrive.

Acclaimed author Anne Lamott in her book *Bird by Bird* states, "Writing is about telling the truth." That's what I aim to do in this book. Tell the truth of my story through courage, clarity, and confidence, sharing the stories of women I've had the honor of coaching and befriending, in the hopes that you too will find, stand in, and share your truth: allowing yourself to define and embody "success," "fulfillment", and "abundance" on your own terms, personally and professionally.

As a career and leadership coach, I've worked with entry-level to C-suite-level professionals as they've navigated the nuances of their career. In that work it is inevitable that the personal life will affect the professional life, and the professional the personal. I've learned that you cannot segment the personal and the professional, even though a consumerist society would aggressively try to convince you otherwise. If we've learned anything over the past couple of years with the pandemic, we are not designed to compartmentalize our lives, shutting off and turning on the core elements of who we are all the time. We are whole beings, fluid, and in desperate need of more harmony and rest in our everyday lives.

Redefining success, living with courage, clarity, and confidence in your career, and by default your life, is messy, nontraditional, complex, and at times can be very challenging. It's not a *place* where you arrive. It's a *process* where you continuously evolve. You're learning to ebb and flow in abundance, not scarcity. Understanding the intentional practice of valuing and exercising your vision and voice.

I want you to treat this book as part inspiration, part guidebook, and part workbook to implement the action steps I have found to be fundamental to career success for women. Let this book help you clear the clutter and serve as a road map that helps you redefine success for yourself, then pursue it.

Before you dig into the chapters ahead, you may be wondering why the steps to redefine success are found in courage, clarity, and confidence. Why those three? Why in that particular order? All great questions!

The framework to redefining success is the process I went through on my own journey. Of course, I did not have language to describe my experience while I was in the thick of it, but after lots of journaling, reading, and self-discovery I was able to pinpoint specific themes. The three that consistently emerged and served as pillars in my pathway to define and pursue success were courage, clarity, and confidence.

I have found that it matters that they go in this order because one builds on top of the other. I've learned firsthand that you cannot have confidence without clarity, and you cannot have clarity without the courage to stop living in the past or future, and come into the present to stand in undeniable awareness. To acknowledge what's not working and audaciously decide to do something about it.

To be more specific, I had to have the *courage* to stop living my life in what I *should* do and start living my life in what I *must* do. I have author Elle Luna to thank for that language from her book, *The Crossroads of Should and Must: Find and Follow Your Passion*. As a Black woman, perfectionist, and professional people-pleaser, I had an uphill battle to fight. The *shoulds* were

EVERYWHERE. Societal, cultural, and familial expectations were loud and clear. I wore myself out seeking to meet and exceed those expectations. I smiled in public and struggled in silence. I was so disconnected from my truest self that at times I felt like a robot, just going through the motions every day. There was a period of time where I cried every day. I open up about this in the pages ahead, but it took courage for me, and later my clients, to give ourselves permission to choose the path of what we *must* do and abandon what everyone else emphatically knew we should be doing with our lives.

Most importantly, stop living to work. We're not waiting for retirement age to enjoy our lives; we're going to excel in our career and lives simultaneously. Not someday, but right now. You do not have to wait to get to a certain place or level in your career or reach a certain income level to have purpose and meaning and fulfillment in your work and life. I know that it sounds contrary to popular belief, but your work can be enjoyable, mission aligned, and you can be compensated well; however, it requires that you drop the expectations and comparison game to embody the boldest, strongest, most courageous version of *yourself*.

As for *clarity* – it's one of the most powerful states of being. To be able to articulate who you are, what matters most to you, to know and understand how to leverage your strengths, and live your life in an unapologetic way that is in alignment with your values. To be aware of and own your unique experiences and zone of genius. It's what we all long for in our everyday lives and that absolutely includes our career.

And when you have clarity, there is conviction – a deep, resounding knowing of what matters most to you and how you want to show up in the world – a conviction that will make even the baby hairs on your body stand up in confidence! *Confidence* is the source of execution. If you are not taking action – struggling with procrastination – it is almost always connected to confidence, linked back to clarity, and a derivative of a lack of courage. A real fear or barrier that is holding you back.

I want to point out that the confidence I am referring to throughout the book is not "fake it till you make it" confidence, or the confidence needed for a specific presentation or meeting at work. The confidence that I am referring to, and which I hope you'll find yourself cultivating as you work through this book, is what I call holistic confidence: confidence that is intrinsic and not predicated on external validation because *you know, value, and trust yourself* to navigate any room, circumstance, or conversation.

As you read the pages ahead and grasp the principles within this book, I hope that you are courageously honest, gain clarity on what you must do, and confidently make each decision in your life and career to honor the strongest, boldest, most courageous version of yourself.

PART

I

Courage

Vulnerability is not weakness; it's our greatest measure of courage.
—Brené Brown

RESISTANCE.

Courage is always preceded by resistance. Often subtle in the beginning, the resistance occurs over time. It manifests itself in different ways in our careers, but some of the most common occurrences are:

- Taking two to three times longer to do common, easy tasks for work
- Letting emails pile up and ignoring them
- Dodging phone calls and Slack messages
- Declining nonessential meetings that you would otherwise attend
- A significant increase in eye-rolling during meetings you do attend
- Allowing yourself to be easily distracted
- Daydreaming
- Procrastination

Avoiding work tasks altogether for as long as possible
_____ (fill in the blank)

Resistance occurs when something is no longer working. That something is out of alignment. The passion is gone. Can't seem to find the meaning in the work. You're doubting the purpose. There's conflict, an incongruence with your values.

You start to question yourself. Wondering if it's you. But you realize it is in fact the job, the culture, the work, the manager – or all four. Maybe life in general just feels off too. You keep finding yourself resisting at every turn, every day. You're realizing that something needs to change. You refuse to accept or comply with work and life "as is" any more. You've had enough of dragging yourself through each day.

You find yourself daydreaming about more. More purpose and meaning. More fulfillment. More autonomy. More financial freedom. More joy. You hope that there is more. And deep down you know that there is more, but you're afraid.

Courage is defined as "the mental or moral strength to venture, persevere, and withstand danger, fear, or difficulty."[1]

You don't know what is beyond the life you've been living. And you're concerned about what will be required of you to experience *more*. You wonder, is it really worth it? Should I take the risk for *more*?

Yes.

Absolutely.

You are worth *more*.

But the requirement is courage.

Courage to step into awareness, take the risk, and be curious.

The common thread that keeps so many of us in resistance and stuck is the misconception that we are the "first" or the "only" to feel the way that we feel. The absence of examples of everyday women who get unstuck are not as visible and prominent as they should be. So, we continue to appear and be perceived as successful or having it together while in the throes of struggle. We view ourselves as less than, weak even, not realizing that vulnerability is the first act of courage.

The fear of admitting the struggle prevents us from opening up and connecting with a community of women with shared experiences. I want to open up dialogue about what has or is currently happening with women in our careers and its impact on our lives as a whole and offer a pathway forward.

Throughout the pages of this book, I share my story and the stories of other women navigating the resistance and moving through courage and clarity, then landing and living in confidence. There is strength in numbers. There is relief in connection. There is courage in conversation. There is healing in community.

You are not alone.

1

The Current State of Women and Work

FOR A WOMAN in today's current climate, it takes courage to go to work every day.

The glass ceiling with all of its dents and cracks still exists. A small fraction of the challenges we deal with are:

- The gender wage gap, where the maximum we earn is 80 cents to each $1 a man makes.
- The Motherhood Penalty,[1] earning just 71 cents to every $1 a father makes.
- The fact that we are expected to be primary caregivers and are severely impacted when caregiving needs arise.
- The lack of support for us in management.
- The failure to promote us into executive leadership roles and how companies ultimately suffer as a result of our absence at the decision-making table.
- We are ignored in meetings at work; worse, we are blatantly undermined and reduced to an "assumed" administrative role.

- We experience overt and covert harassment and discrimination, of all kinds, at work.
- We walk into toxic work cultures and the obnoxious bro-culture that unbelievably still exists.
- We have to navigate the inequities with work on top of the actual duties of our job, and let's not forget the pressure to deliver on unrealistic goals while we "smile more" and "consider our tone."

In this chapter I *attempt* to give an overview of the current state of affairs for women and work. I carefully chose the word "attempt." There are so many instances, circumstances, experiences, perspectives, and stories that there could be an entire catalogue of books on the current state of affairs for women and work. There's no way I or any single person could capture it all. My effort, therefore, is to highlight the commonalities of shared experiences and some of the most prevalent challenges. Having context, shared language, and perspective from the same angle will illuminate the importance of the framework provided in the chapters ahead.

The Rules of Engagement Are Changing

When the pandemic hit, it further exposed, highlighted, and underscored the inequities women face at work and in their day-to-day lives, from the massive, forceful exit of women due to caregiving responsibilities to exacerbating the demand for women to deliver peak performance and save companies – all while working from home. It was and continues to be problematic and detrimental, not just to women but to society as a whole.

Women are in a battle that will require new rules of engagement when it comes to the way we work. Women's fundamental rights are at stake both inside and outside the office. From the pandemic to the recent Supreme Court Roe v. Wade verdict, there are and continue to be clear indicators that we, as women, have to do something differently if we want to be seen, heard, and paid, and to continue to pave the way for other women to choose and fulfill their own definition of success.

And by doing something differently, I don't mean hustling harder, changing who you are to fit someone else's expectations, dumbing down yourself or your qualifications, or increasing your tolerance amid toxic work cultures. I'm talking about something more drastic, impactful, and meaningful.

I'm talking about quitting any job that does not respect, value, or support your work and the progression of your career. If companies can do it without us, *let them try*, period.

Far too many women are in abusive relationships with work and it's time that you break up for once and for all. Breaking up with a toxic work relationship, manager, or environment looks like putting yourself first, knowing your professional and personal value, advocating for yourself, and making the decision to no longer accept anything other than a healthy organization that compensates you well, offers an aligned culture that shares similar values, and that appreciates your time, talent, and experience. It's not easy. It's absolutely not convenient, but it is necessary.

Let's stop making excuses and staying in positions that are silently – or not so silently – killing not only our careers but ourselves, literally. The physical and mental health issues we experience due to the chronic stress associated with work, a toxic work culture, and a terrible boss are unacceptable. Even if it seems impossible, know that you do have options. If you need a strategy for how to quit well, do a quick good search for my latest Ted-Talk, "How to Quit Without Ruining Your Career".

The Way We Are Expected to Work Is Becoming a Public Health Crisis

US Surgeon General Vivek Murthy released the *Surgeon General's Framework for Workplace Mental Health and Well-being* report in

2022. The report documents the severe impacts that toxic work environments can have on our physical and mental health. The report states, *In fact, chronic stress has also been linked to a higher risk of developing diseases such as high blood pressure, high cholesterol, heart disease, obesity, cancer, and autoimmune diseases. Such stress can also contribute to mental and behavioral health challenges, including depression, anxiety, suicidal ideation, and substance misuse, and can have negative impacts on the mental health of the children and families of workers."*[2]

According to CBS News, this report is the "first time the Surgeon General has explicitly linked job factors such as low wages, discrimination, harassment, overwork, long commutes and other factors to chronic physical health conditions like heart disease and cancer. Work-related stress can also lead to mental health conditions including depression and anxiety . . ."[3]

The pandemic put a spotlight on workplace cultures and practices that have taken a toll on workers and their families for far too long – I read "workers" as women, in particular. This report is not just about frontline workers, as so many reports often highlight. It specifically calls out all companies who fail to meet what the Surgeon General has identified as the *Five Essentials for Workplace Mental Health & Well-Being*, which includes the following components outlined in the report (and illustrated in Figure 1.1):

Protection from Harm

- Prioritize workplace physical and psychological safety
- Enable adequate rest
- Normalize and support mental health
- Operationalize Diversity, Equity, Inclusion, and Accessibility (DEIA) norms, policies, and programs

Connection and Community

- Create cultures of inclusion and belonging
- Cultivate trusted relationships
- Foster collaboration and teamwork

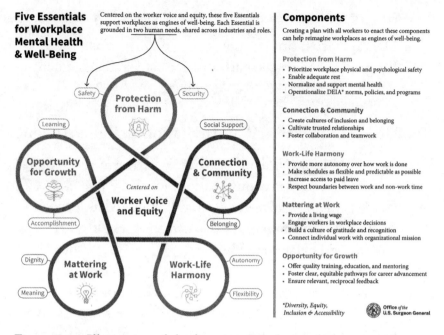

Figure 1.1 Illustration of the five essentials for workplace mental health and well-being.

Source: https://www.hhs.gov/sites/default/files/workplace-mental-health-well-being.pdf

Work-Life Harmony

- Provide more autonomy over how work is done
- Make schedules as flexible and predictable as possible
- Increase access to paid leave
- Respect boundaries between work and nonwork time

Mattering at Work

- Provide a living wage
- Engage workers in workplace decisions
- Build a culture of gratitude and recognition
- Connect individual work with the organizational mission

Opportunity for Growth

- Offer quality training, education, and mentoring
- Foster clear, equitable pathways for career advancement
- Ensure relevant, reciprocal feedback

Knowledge Is Power and an Invitation to Take Action

If you do not have a standard for where you decide to exchange your time and talent for compensation, let those five essentials be a *starting place*. A common question I am asked as a coach is, "How do I know if a company or department is healthy? How do I know it's a good place to work?"

My immediate response is to go look at the executive and senior leadership teams. If there is an absence of diversity – gender, racial, socioeconomic, or otherwise – your voice is likely absent from the room. Pay attention to the diversity of the team you'll be working with day-to-day. During your interview, ask every person about diversity, equity, and inclusion efforts and pay close attention to how they respond.

Second, do your due diligence. Speak with employees at the company at different levels – entry to senior – and inquire about their experience working for the company. A quick LinkedIn search can help you identify individuals you can reach out to and connect with to learn more. You can also ask HR about the general percentage of turnover and specifically about the percentage of turnover for employees who identify as women within the company. You may want to be more specific and ask those questions directly to teams you'll be working with in your role. If HR won't share, you can typically find some data on job search sites online.

Third, ask to review their workplace policies and handbook *before* you accept the offer. Check to see if their policies address concerns that are most important to you. At the very least, make sure they include elements of the workplace health and well-being framework.

Last, but not least, ask questions that you want answered during the interview or at the offer phase of the process. Ask open-ended questions rather than close-ended questions with yes or no answers. For example, you would not ask, "Do you have a work from home policy?" Instead, ask, "What is your work from home policy? How do employees typically utilize the policy?" Phrasing your question this way makes a big difference that can provide you with more information and insight.

The workplace is shifting and it will shift again, but how work impacts our health and well-being is a matter that can become a public health crisis if there isn't continual progress and change. The change starts with us, and who we choose as our employer. And the research shows that we, as women, are making better choices.

A Snapshot of the Research

The *2022 Women and Workplace Report*[4] by Lean In and McKinsey & Company calls out a key observation about women and work. I won't call it a trend because I don't think this is a short-term change. I think it's a long-term change with impact that improves the workplace for all employees, not just women. It's called the "Great Break-Up." As defined by the report, the Great Break-Up means that "women are demanding more from work and they're leaving in unprecedented numbers to get it." Women are indeed breaking up with bad employers, toxic work cultures, and horrific managers. I. AM. HERE. FOR. IT. The report states, "In the past year, women leaders have switched jobs at the highest rates we've ever seen."

And if you're not leaving your job just yet, I bet you're engaged in quiet quitting until you're ready for your next move. Quiet

Quitting is the act of physically showing up to work but not being fully present and engaged. It's doing only what is essential or necessary in the job – basically the job you were hired to do sans the "above and beyond" (i.e. working early or late, committee work, additional projects or assignments, working tirelessly until you exceed your boss's expectations). It's letting go of the extra, also known as "other duties as assigned" and not delivering all that you are capable of delivering.

The irony for me is why is it called "quiet quitting" instead of "doing my job"? Hello somebody! Hustle culture has us thinking that we if we just do our jobs, we are not doing enough. Since when did the compensation and promotion requirements become a competition about who can sacrifice the most of themselves? It's crazy! Sacrificing so much of our lives for a company that can let us go at any time and replace us tomorrow just doesn't make sense, but we're doing it because we've been told and believe it's the only way to become successful.

But seriously the point in getting to quiet quitting is that you know there is something that isn't working. You're not receiving feedback, there's no talk of career progression within the company, or you're constantly met with more you need to do to be considered for a promotion. You realize that the contributions you make are not recognized or valued. Maybe you've come to realize you're not as passionate about the work or the company culture and team just aren't a good fit. It's the scenario where you know the breakup is coming, the clock is ticking, it's just a matter of when.

On the flip side there is another term: "quiet firing." Quiet Firing[5] is when employers covertly push out employees by neglecting to promote, compensate, and develop individuals within their organization. I would venture to say women, particularly women of color, are more likely to experience quiet firing. In this scenario, you are nailing the "above and beyond," taking on additional responsibilities, arriving early and staying late, yet you're not getting the feedback you need, there's no additional compensation, and no plan for career advancement. WTH? Make it make sense.

I think quiet firing is the catalyst for quiet quitting.

When both phenomena, quiet firing and quiet quitting, emerged on LinkedIn, they were the hot topics of conversation for both employers and employees. Since February 2020, more than 1.067 MILLION women[6] have been absent from the workforce and they haven't been returning. Leading the "breakup" are Black women who are done with "microaggressions, belittling, and burnout" according to *Business Insider*.[7] In fact, the article continues, "The percentage of Black women in the labor force – which includes everything from corporate work to service jobs – dropped from 60.5% in 2019 to 58.8% in 2020, the largest annual decrease for the group, according to the Department of Labor. The participation rate remained unchanged in 2021."[8] Where are they going? Entrepreneurship.

On the opposite side of the spectrum, for the women who are choosing to stay, there has been a slight increase in women's advancement in leadership roles, but before we call it a win, let's be sure to acknowledge that those leadership roles continue to involve limitations in seniority and are constricted by bias, harassment, racial tensions, and gender inequities.

Burnout Is an Invitation to Evolve

Regardless of which end of the pendulum you find yourself on, toxic burnout is the underlying collective experience we are all having regardless of our age, industry, marital status, or caregiving responsibility. The burnout at times feels all-consuming and we are certain that a crash in our professional and personal lives is inevitable. We are tired in a different and deeper way in our souls during a pivotal period that will shape our future as women. That different way, you may ask, is a way that a nap won't fix, a vacation won't cure, and getting a new job won't quite resolve.

We're in a season of burnout and trauma that requires *us* to evolve. Not into something or someone different, but to evolve into the boldest, strongest, most courageous version of ourselves. To lay things down, to say no, to go slow, and to prioritize what is most important. It will require recreation, which I refer to as *re-creation*: time to create and be creative, to make connection, and grow community. That is what I hope you find in this book.

As a coach, I focus on supporting and helping women evolve. My focus on career development and advancement for women is not coincidental. Women's careers are largely the epicenter of community, connection, change, and of what I believe to be the mission we've all been striving to achieve: a new definition and standard for success.

Want to share your thoughts with me?

 Join the conversation and download worksheets from this chapter over on the Courage, Clarity, and Confidence website: www.courage clarityconfidence.com.

2

Courage + Risk

YOU WANT THE courage to take the risk.

You want the unfiltered clarity about who you are and permission to fully explore what you are truly capable of doing.

You want the confidence to pursue and embody the strongest, bravest, boldest version of yourself.

We all desire on some level to be bold and audacious, and to explore our curiosity. It's a risky decision.

Unfortunately, as women, especially in our careers, we are subconsciously taught and consciously reminded that "traditionally" we cannot afford to be risk takers. There are systems that penalize women for taking risks, from having children, to taking a sabbatical.

We are told directly or indirectly that it will cost us our career, our reputation, our financial future if we are too strong, too direct, too feminine, or _____ (fill in the blank). The list is long and exhaustive. Not to mention that if we can push past the fear of the backlash, there is an absence of support once we do take the risk.

The choice to abandon the expectations placed on us, discover our own authentic desires, and pursue alignment with the vision we have for our personal lives and our careers is a messy battle. And as if it weren't hard enough dealing with the external barriers, the internal barrages of imposter syndrome, self-criticism, guilt, or worthiness when making ourselves a priority causes analysis paralysis, self-doubt, and procrastination. There are very few examples in everyday life of women who have done what we are seeking to do.

Courage is stifled in our careers in particular from the very beginning and we spend a significant amount of time and energy wrestling with the "right way" to show up at work. We are forced to fraction ourselves for what is considered a culturally normative level of career success. And if you are a woman of color, the weight is crushing.

It's no wonder we are burned out, stuck in a position that barely scratches the surface of the talent we possess, and are leaving the traditional pathway of work for entrepreneurial or freelance work. We are seeking some solace. Our careers take up a huge chunk of our lives. Nothing accounts for more of our lifetime than our career.

Why is it such a detriment to society to be able to enjoy work, be compensated well, be valued for our unique perspective and skill set, bring our whole selves to the table, and you know, not be harassed, silenced, or treated like we're invisible?

In this chapter I share my own personal story of how I decided to take the risk and bet on myself. The amount of courage it took paled in comparison to the stress and anxiety of being in a role and environment where my intelligence, value, and contributions were undermined. I gave myself permission to choose myself. I hope you'll find yourself in elements of my story and find a way to give yourself permission to take your own leap of faith.

Taking the Leap

After a failed search for a new assistant director in our department, I decided to apply. The chair of the search committee told me point-blank, "If you had applied when this position first became available we wouldn't even be in this situation." I didn't know what to say in response. I didn't have a legitimate reason why I didn't apply. My plate was already full and I was doing director-level work. I didn't feel inclined to sign up for more work. But after some consideration, and what I assumed to be encouragement, I applied. Within a week I had a phone interview. I thought it went well. I was prepared. No surprises. I expected an on-site interview. I did not get one. I was shocked.

When I later inquired about why I was not selected to move forward for the assistant director role, my assistant vice president told me it wouldn't be favorable to be promoted again within such a short period of time. I had been promoted once by this organization within an 18-month period.

The feedback from my boss, a vice president, made me question my ambition and ultimately myself. I was doing the work, more than my fair share, and getting the results. I valued my work and was making an impact. It was clear I had all of the qualities (not to mention qualifications) of a promising, effective leader. Yet the message I got from my boss was that my aspirations needed to be tempered down. In our conversation, she went so far as to suggest that I be placed on a pseudo professional development plan so that my ability to "be a good leader could be cultivated." I refer to it as a pseudo professional development plan because the workbook printout she gave me looked so generic. I obliged my curiosity and did a Google search for "professional development plan workbook" and as fate would have it, the document she gave me was the first link in my Google search results. Talk about TACKY. I literally wanted to throw the whole thing in the trash. Honestly, I don't know why I didn't. I think the disappointment overwhelmed me in the moment. The fact that I was being put through a "professional development" plan belittled the work I was already doing.

Isn't that almost always the case? That in order to move up to the next level, you need to "be developed" even though you've clearly been doing the work at the next level and beyond for months if not years? Personally, I think it's a stall tactic and full of empty promises. Very rarely is it ever a genuine attempt to help you grow and develop. Yet we nod and agree to the "plan" and withhold our honest feelings at the expense of not being labeled the "angry Black woman" at work. What stereotypical label do you feel like you have to manage at work? Whatever it is, I know it's exhausting.

I'll never forget one particular day when my office phone rang. It was a Friday, mid-morning, and I was sitting at my desk trying to sort through a busy week. I wasn't going to answer my office phone. I was tired. It had been a long week already, but on a whim, I answered with a ring or two to spare. What I hoped would be a quick call instead left me asking WTF!? On the line was a peer from another organization calling to congratulate me on an award my office received. She wanted to ask me some questions regarding the implementation of our program and how we were able to achieve such impressive results. Guess who had no idea about any submission for an award, nothing about winning an award, and was not credited in any way for the work?

Me.

So you mean, my work is out here winning awards, but my boss thinks it's too soon to promote me for award-winning work? Make it make sense.

In fact, instead of promoting me, she decided to hire a man. And not just any man, a man who, within his first couple of weeks of work, walked into my office for our 1:1, sat down, and said, "I need you to teach me everything you know. I don't know what I'm doing." I was trying my best to hide my disbelief. I literally felt sick to my stomach. I had to temper down my rage. I clutched my pen TIGHTLY and took a deep breath.

I shouldn't have been surprised by his behavior based on his interview; it was clear he was all about the optics with little tangible evidence of his own results. But I was astonished at his boldness and expectation that I would actually oblige his request. Not to mention the perception that we could somehow accomplish his request in a 30- to 45-minute meeting. I made the mistake of assuming he might use the time to share his vision, management style, and inquire about the needs of my business unit.

And before we get too far into this particular story, it's important to note that this man was hired by a woman. The same woman who told me it was too soon for a promotion. A woman of color, to be exact. Hearing this feedback from someone who looked like me made me more upset, sad really, than if it had come from a "Todd." I would have expected it from Todd, but I totally didn't expect this experience from another woman, one who looked like me. The same woman who assured me in my interview that she would help advance my career so I could be in a position like hers one day.

> Todd: The universal name for a privileged white man with zero interest in supporting or elevating anyone other than someone who looks and thinks just like him. His agenda is preserving patriarchy and inequality.

It was a double hit to my psyche: first, although I was qualified, it was frowned upon to be promoted within an undisclosed time period; and second, to see a woman of color fully submit herself to the patriarchal structure and hire a man who was not as qualified as I was (or the other some of the other candidates) shocking. Then to watch her double down on her submission to the patriarchal mindset by telling me I needed to be professionally developed instead.

The audacity.

The irony.

It all became clear in a meeting a couple of months later where she and her new hire told me that due to the success of the program in my business unit, they wanted me to broadly expand it – more than doubling the staff and offerings of the already severely under-resourced program.

When I inquired about the logistics and requested an increase of financial and human resources to implement the plan she envisioned for the expansion, she said directly, without answers to my questions, "We will do this with or without you." I'll never forget those words nor the look on the new guy's face. He was just as stunned as I was at her arrogance and disrespect for all of my hard work.

I was ready to flip my desk and let her have it. I said nothing. After the meeting I typed up my resignation letter and considered whether I could actually quit that day. Financially, it wasn't an option, but it was going to be very soon. I started to prepare an exit strategy. I was done.

It was literally in that meeting that my courage shifted its trajectory. Instead of the courage to advance in leadership within that organization, I immediately had the courage to quit. I wanted to bet on myself. I wanted to take the risk. I had the conviction to do so. I knew that nothing in that job or that type of leadership was going to change anytime soon. If I was going to work that hard for someone else, I wanted to find a way to work that hard for myself and get paid for it.

It would take just a few more months to actually pull the trigger and I courageously quit. I couldn't have been prouder to submit that letter of resignation even though I almost threw up while doing so. That's the thing about courage – it's never convenient, or easy, and often takes you by surprise with what it teaches you.

I found the courage to take the risk. I gave myself permission to decide to honor myself and let go, knowing that I was capable of handling what would come next. I knew I deserved more.

Give Yourself Permission

Where do you need to give yourself permission? I first heard of the concept of "permission slips" from Brené Brown in her book *Braving the Wilderness*. Of course, you're familiar with the concept of permission slips from grade school, but it wasn't until reading her words that I realized how powerful permission slips would be in adulthood.

According to Brené,

> *Permission slips give us a practical and familiar way to think about what might get in the way of us talking about how we feel, asking for what we need, or trying something new. Their primary function is to serve as an explicit intention setting.*[1]

The illusion of perfection was in my way. As a recovering perfectionist, I like to think of permission in terms of the ability to mess up or fail – personally and publicly – as acknowledging the messiness of what comes in the process of doing something new. Something like getting really honest and candid about what you feel, what's not working, and what you truly want. It takes courage internally and externally to admit that life is not what you thought it was going to be, the career path isn't right for you, the job isn't what you thought it would be, especially when friends and family are watching.

I want you to give yourself a permission slip. I want you to honor yourself by acknowledging how you truly feel, what you need, and where you need permission to take a risk. You can create a permission slip using the following template or write it out in a journal.

Permission Slip Template

I, _____ [insert your name], give myself permission to feel
_____.

I recognize that I truly need _____
_____.

I want to take the risk, to bet on myself, so that I can _____
_____
_____
_____.

This is important to me because _____
_____
_____.

I give myself permission to _____
_____.

I give myself permission to pursue these goals with abandon – without guilt or shame – recognizing that growth is messy and unpredictable. I promise to be patient with my own process and to honor myself with respect and love, as I would a good friend.

One small step I can take to honor my decision right now is _____
_____.

In six months I will have accomplished _____
_____.

In a year I will have accomplished _____

_____.

I believe in myself, I trust myself, and I know that I am capable of what I desire. —Me

You may not be quite ready to fill out this permission slip – and that's OK. Just knowing that you want to do this is a good place to start. And even if you don't know what you're looking for right now, I hope you also recognize that this permission slip is not a one-time deal. You can come back to this again and again throughout this process, to continually honor the person you are becoming.

I am asking you to get reacquainted with yourself. If you're like me, it had been a very long time since I connected with my true self. The process to meet her was terrifying some days. It required a lot of personal confession, admission, and thoughts of "you can never say this out loud" reprimands, but I was determined to be honest with myself and give myself permission where I needed it.

After all, I had done everything everyone else told me to do and ended up miserable. I deserved to listen to myself and not apologize for the chaos of not having it all figured out. I surmised that exploring myself couldn't possibly be worse than sitting with the uncertainty, frustration, and anxiety I was already encountering on my couch night after night.

I realized in those moments that the only person that could save me was me. The only person who could make me happy was me. The only way I would be fulfilled in life was if I understood what I needed to be fulfilled. This wasn't about anyone else, not my boss, the new guy, or the job. It was about me.

Want to share your thoughts with me?

 Join the conversation and download work-sheets from this chapter over on the Courage, Clarity, and Confidence website: www.courage clarityconfidence.com.

3

Courage + Curiosity

SOCIETY AND CULTURE – in very overt, but also very covert ways – teach us as women not to value our voices, our needs, our own feminine power. Family and friends can tie you up with expectations, pressure to be something they were or were not, or challenge you to become the version of the person they want or need you to be. For so many of us, we get tangled up in people-pleasing tendencies. We find ourselves engaged in guilt-ridden behaviors, in sacrifice for others all the time, so it's no wonder there's a disconnect from what we really feel, need, or want.

In my twenties, I found myself neck-deep in wanting to appear successful, put together, and on top of things. Like so many other women, I was governing my life by the concept of "The Clock" that apparently only exists for women. You know, the one that starts ticking the day you graduate from college: find a good job, get married, buy a house, have kids. The "American Dream" is synonymous with success. But it shouldn't be. You need to have your own real definition of "success" independent of a job, husband, kids, new house, and nice cars. Those things can be a part of success, but that's nowhere close to a complete definition. Yet we often still measure a significant portion of our worth, value, and decisions on this uniform, monochromatic definition of "success."

In this chapter, I share my transition from college graduation to career, pinpointing the moment I realized that I had been chasing an illusion of success. I share how I stumbled my way through a wilderness of uncertainty and how curiosity became the guide I needed to transform my life and career.

Pursuing the "American Dream"

I graduated college in four years by taking classes every summer except my freshman year. While tackling that four-year timeline, I got a job on campus, participated in campus organizations and activities, secured scholarships, and stayed out of trouble (I was too tired for anything else).

When I left my parents' house at 18 years old, I was on a mission to prove to them and myself that I could be an independent young woman. And for the most part, I was. I was resourceful and responsible. I did well academically, socially, and was navigating the nuances of being a young professional woman. I observed how hard my parents worked to give us better and more. They were examples of what is possible with sacrifice, determination, and hard work. I was NOT going to let their work be in vain. I understood the assignment at an early age. I focused myself on the expectations of my parents and the cultural expectations of being a successful black woman, turning those expectations into personal goals. I was relentless. And if you couldn't tell, I was a people-pleasing perfectionist who found validation in the outward praise of my accomplishments.

I completed my master's degree right after my undergraduate degree, and within a year and a half of graduating with my master's degree, I started working for a company that was on my five-year career goals list. Shortly after, with the help of my parents, I was able to purchase my first home. I even bought a new car. All that was missing was the husband and kids. I was checking all of the boxes everyone told me I needed to if I wanted to be happy, if I wanted to be considered "successful".

In the evenings I would work late, volunteer, or hang out with friends. Eventually those evenings turn into watching tv on my couch for a few hours before going to bed. Somewhere along this successful path I realized I wasn't happy. I didn't enjoy my job anymore. The house was nice, but it was empty. I just didn't feel like myself. There was a period of time where I came home and cried on the couch after work so frustrated by the tension and anxiety I felt: to almost have it all yet feel like you have nothing you truly want all at the same time. I was lost in the seas of uncertainty, and the waves of anxiety made for some very long and sleepless nights.

I can remember repeatedly reminding myself that I should feel satisfied, happy, and successful with a job, a new house, a new car, and husband prospects. I should have been celebrating the check marks on my "success" checklist: go to college, get a great job, meet the guy, get married, buy the house, have kids . . . You. Know. This. Story. We are fed it from birth, it seems. But things just weren't adding up.

I felt guilty for not feeling happy, satisfied. And as a Black woman, the opportunity to have this "American Dream" was a priviledge. I believed it was what my parents sacrificed and worked so hard to give to me and my three sisters. Once I realized that running the rat race of chasing and accomplishing what everyone else wanted didn't quite add up to the life I wanted, I had to sit with that and make sense of it.

While I maintained the outward appearance of "having it all and being happy," I wrestled internally. Those nights on the couch went from watching TV to reflecting, reading, and journaling.

As an Enneagram 3: The Achiever, I was motivated by productivity, accomplishment, and success. In my limited thinking at the time, I thought a possible answer was getting a new job.

A new challenge.

A new environment.

A fresh start.

Surely, that would be helpful. And it was . . . a nice distraction. I had new problems to solve, I felt like I had a sense of belonging and necessity, but what I realized, very quickly, was that I was in the same "job" with a little bit more money. I was the same person in a new physical environment. The truth is changing my job was not the answer I was seeking. I would still come home after work every single day and lie on the couch. Some days I cried. Other days I cried more.

One cold, hard fact that I learned during that season: You will continue in the same "job" unless you confront the truth about what you really need. And here is a hint, what you really need won't come from an external source. Read that again. As career-oriented women, our jobs become pillars of an unhealthy identity. We'll reduce our value to company names, job titles, and salaries if we're not careful.

I love books and find trips to my local bookstore cathartic when I feel lost and confused. Books always have a way of unlocking things for me. During one of my trips, I would scan the shelves with thousands of titles until one captivated my attention. During one of my trips, I found Craig Groeschel's book *Chazown: Define Your Vision. Pursue Your Passion. Live Your Life on Purpose*. The title of the book was exactly what I wanted to do. I dug in deep. I was determined to get out of the fog I found myself in each day.

As I did the work, what transpired was an introduction: I was meeting my truest self for the first time. I was so well acquainted with others' perceptions of me and the perception I wanted others to have of me, but I had not intentionally connected to the real, authentic, version of who I was independent of those perceptions. I didn't truly know who I was independent of the "shoulds" of others.

What I realized during that time is in large part the foundation of this book. I needed to locate myself, discover who I was, and decide who I wanted to be and what I wanted to do. I needed to redefine success for myself and then live by that definition.

All those nights on the couch were indicators that I was lacking fulfillment. I felt like I was playing a game of cat and mouse – perpetually chasing a status and appearance. I had the mindset that if I followed all of the advice, played by the rules, and worked hard, success would be inevitable. Now where was it? What I found instead was frustration, doubt, and a lot of questions. I was so caught up in what I was told "success" should be that I never even considered that for me it could and would be something totally different from anything I had seen up close and personal. And that it was ok for my definition to be different.

Success is about alignment.

Alignment is defined as "a state of agreement or cooperation among persons, groups, nations, etc., with a common cause or viewpoint."[1] It's about being in an alliance and agreement with who you are and knowing that as you move into alignment with your most authentic self, the right career, relationships, and opportunities will line up for you.

If you can manage to be so honest and transparent with yourself that you can learn to move in alignment with yourself without seeking to meet the expectations of external cultural or familial voices, and reframe failure as learning, you will have an overwhelming abundance of courage, clarity, and confidence.

I know it to be possible because it is the story of my own life and the lives of so many of my clients. Hindsight is always 20/20. *I realized that my perfectionist and people-pleasing tendencies caused me to abandon curiosity for control. When you abandon curiosity for control, you are creating barriers to being successful.*

Reaching a level of self-actualization is not a one-time deal. Alignment is not a singular destination; you can't just "arrive" at alignment and stay there. It is a continual evolutionary process. It requires sustained dedication and effort. It is a practice, a process, a commitment to oneself. And that process starts with a permission slip to be honest.

The Latin root word for honesty is *honestus* and the original sense of the word was "honor, respectability." Talk about a loaded definition, whew.

Let's give ourselves another permission slip here. A permission slip to honor ourselves by treating ourselves with respectability.

The pathway to clarity and to having more confidence first requires courage to be curious. To go after what you truly want, to receive the answers you're desperately seeking, all starts with your ability to honor yourself right where you are – in the midst of frustration, disappointment, confusion, or uncertainty – *and* treat yourself with dignity. To recognize you have value – intrinsically and extrinsically. Give yourself grace and space to take things one day at a time and accept that you do not need to be perfect, have it all together, or constantly be busy. Give yourself a permission slip to live to incorporate work, not work to live.

It is OK to say your life and career, as they are right now, are not working. As frustrating as that can be, give yourself permission not to know the answer. Have the courage to submit yourself to the process of curiosity and exploration, which we will do together in the next section of this book.

Both may sound like a luxury – to have time to explore and be curious – but I assure you both are necessary and you learn that taking the time is nonnegotiable. You may feel like you don't have the time due to current circumstances, demands, expectations, but what you truly don't have time for is 5, 10, or 25+ years living out of alignment with yourself.

I've had conversations with more established women at the top of their careers who are planning to explore what we call a second act. A second act is a transition in your career to doing what you truly *want* to do – after you've done what is *expected* of you. The common theme I noticed working with these women is that they wished they had made the pivot to what they wanted to do earlier in their careers. They wished they had had the courage and tools to turn their heart work into full-time work. They wanted a career that honored their lifestyle, values, and purpose.

Curiosity is perceived as a luxury for women, especially for women of color. The demands of work and home don't allow for exploration and risk, but without both there is absolutely no fulfillment. In my work with clients, I find that having curiosity, and the opportunity to follow where the curiosity leads you, is met with high expenses. We're so tied up with having to work two and three times as hard to be seen and heard, navigating male-dominated career paths, archaic company cultures, grappling with the impact of gender pay and wealth gaps, meeting the demands of caregiving, and more – the list is long and the costs are high. When do we have the time and how do we afford it?

Knowing that women can lose up to $1M or more in their career automatically makes the idea of having time for curiosity unimaginable. Not to mention that being in a consumerist society, where engaging in thinking for yourself, refuting hustle culture, or doing something not directly tied to achievement, status, or money is viewed as being lazy, aloof, or worse, having a lack of drive or ambition. We live in a period of human history where the key components that make us fully human and healthy are strongly discouraged under the guise of not having enough time.

I fundamentally believe that curiosity is right in line with tier one of Maslow's Hierarchy of Needs – right next to air, food, and shelter. As a coach, one of the most powerful tools I've learned to use in my professional and personal life is curiosity. When I was working toward one of my coaching certifications I was enthralled as we learned about neuroplasticity and curiosity. Neuroplasticity, in the simplest definition, is the brain's comprehensive ability to create new pathways of learning and being, whereas curiosity is the genuine desire and willingness to explore and learn something new.

Over the last decade, I have coached early career and executive-level professionals. The pivotal elements of every effective coaching relationship are the awareness, desire, willingness, to learn and change – and belief in our power to do so. There is a commitment to oneself and a trust that letting go of one thing will help you grasp what is next. The one thing I know for sure is that defining success for yourself is largely about unlearning and exploring, then identifying who we are, who we want to be, and the impact we want to make in the world through our work.

So let's take that permission slip to be honest and abandon control for curiosity. Let's start by getting curious about ourselves. It's time to reconnect with ourselves and get clear on who we are and our significance. It's the only pathway to alignment.

Want to share your thoughts with me?

 Join the conversation and download worksheets from this chapter over on the Courage, Clarity, and Confidence website: www.courage clarityconfidence.com.

PART

II

Clarity

It is so important to take time for yourself and find clarity. The most important relationship is the one you have with yourself.

—Diane Von Furstenberg

CLARITY IS A superpower.

Clarity is defined as the "quality or state of being clear," according to *Merriam-Webster*, and the definition of *clear* is "free from obscurity or ambiguity: easily understood."[1]

It's the birthplace of confidence.

When we don't have it, we worry, we feel frustrated, and doubt overwhelms us. I believe that is why many women struggle in their careers and leadership.

I don't know about you, but when I am clear about something it's hard to change my mind. Getting to a place of clarity can be frustrating and emotionally draining. It requires us to stop seeking answers externally and instead pursue the answers internally. This is especially hard for us as women because we are made to feel that our intuition cannot and shouldn't be trusted and our voice is not valued. We are rarely ever asked what we think or want and on the rare occasion that we are asked, our answers are dismissed, overlooked, ignored, taken, or twisted.

The interesting thing about clarity is that sometimes we do know exactly what we want, but what hinders us is that we don't believe we are worthy or enough for what we desire, and the last thing we want is confirmation of that belief.

And sometimes the problem is that we don't know how to articulate what we truly desire because it's buried under so much *stuff*. So we play it safe, assimilating into the cultural norms around us, minimizing our feelings, and/or even ignoring our own selves, stifling our very own careers and dreams. We self-protect from toxic work environments. And when there are opportunities that suggest we are enough, that validate our voice and perspective, we don't believe it. We challenge it. We downplay it. We doubt our capability. Imposter syndrome often appears. It's a hard, vicious mindset cycle.

As a former people-pleaser and perfectionist, my answer to what I wanted sought to match what I thought the other person expected of me, or sought to exceed the expectations someone had of me. I wanted to be seen as successful, accomplished, and polished. I was taught that those attributes are what get you far in life. Those attributes helped people to see more than the *color of my skin*. Worthiness was inextricably connected to validation from what others thought about me. I don't know about you, but living by the opinions and expectations of others was its own version of hell. The internal voice I heard was critical, accusatory, and verbally abusive. If you've dealt with perfectionism, you can understand. I didn't grow up with those voices from my parents, loved ones, or friends, but I did grow up being praised for all that I did that was right or admirable. As a little girl, and for any child for that matter, I craved that attention and affirmation. Those were my love languages. Failure wasn't even in my vocabulary.

It wasn't until I exhausted myself chasing the things that I thought I should – college, salaried job immediately after school, home ownership, husband and kids – that I realized I wasn't satisfied. I wasn't happy and felt guilty for not being happy. I checked off so many boxes, but there were still so many unchecked. The ones that mattered most. Critical things like knowing what made *me* happy, knowing my purpose, being comfortable with not being good at something, failing at something, releasing control for curiosity, and more.

Practicing self-compassion and pinpointing what makes us who we are should always be independent of external achievements. Continuously affirming those truths is how we combat this epidemic with our mindset. It is critical for your professional and personal success to *identify*, *accept*, and *honor* what makes you who you are and know that it is *more than enough*.

Courage prompts us to seek out clarity. Clarity requires us to explore our strengths, values, and experiences as guidance and markers of direction. As we reconnect to ourselves, a conviction about who we are and what we believe stirs within us, illustrating a vision of our purpose and informing our mission. That conviction cultivates confidence.

In this section of our journey together, I want to invite you into purposeful self-reflection, self-awareness, and accountability. We're going to explore your values, strengths, experiences, and more to help you gain the clarity you need to be confident.

4

Clarity Framework

WHEN I WORK with clients one-on-one or in one of my courses, we will always go through a series of exercises focused on awareness, evaluation, reconnection, and direction. I believe those four main areas create a path to clarity. With so many different demands, expectations, and microaggressions bombarding our minds every day, we have to come into the awareness of where we are and learn to name the challenges that we are facing. Then it's important to evaluate the impact of those challenges and determine what we need to do to address those barriers.

Next is a process of reconnection where I lead clients through activities that allow them to regain trust with their intuition, values, and voice. Last, but not least, I hold space for my clients to set the direction and next steps to take action and move forward with results. I serve as my client's coach, advisor, confidante, and cheerleader. I stand by the belief that my clients are their own experts and I have the privilege of coming alongside them as their thought-partner while they walk through a transformative journey in their idenity and career.

When we are constantly in unhealthy work cultures with such a high number of unprepared and underdeveloped managers and leaders, it's hard not to question yourself, which can spiral into a place of perpetual self-doubt and produce a lack of clarity and absolutely tank confidence. We lose the sound of our own voice and become silent, simply going through the motions to keep the peace and the bills paid. I read a quote recently on Instagram from Robin Clark that illustrates this complexity where we as women far too often find ourselves: *"Your silence enables people to treat you poorly which is a huge reason girls are taught to not speak up for ourselves, say no, or ever be angry . . . no matter what your good girl conditioning taught you – you did not come here to abandon yourself to be a good (albeit enabling) partner to others."*—*@loverobinclark*[1]

The ASCEND Method

It wasn't until this book that I developed an actual name for the method I use with my clients, even though I have been using the process with clients for years. It's called the ASCEND Practice. It's an acronym that stands for the following components:

- Acknowledge what is no longer working
- Study your strengths
- Connect with your values
- Explore your experiences
- Nurture your voice
- Determine to embody the strongest, boldest, most courageous version of yourself

The definition of the word "ascend" is to move upward, to rise from a lower level or degree, and to succeed – and that is exactly what happens as my clients, and now you too, walk through this method.

Remember when I mentioned Maslow's Hierarchy of Needs back in the beginning of the book? Figure 4.1 shows the hierarchy.

Figure 4.1   Maslow's hierarchy of needs
Source: https://simplypsychology.org/maslow.html

You can think of the ASCEND Practice as a similar pyramid with the **A** of the ASCEND Practice at the bottom of the pyramid, then move up as you progress through the method. This process is parallel to the psychological and physiological process to self-actualization, but within the context of your career. The method is the framework or process to gain clarity, confidence, and redefine success. The process allows you to make the mindset shift from scarcity to abundance, limitations to freedom, and from perceived success to true success. Figure 4.2 shows what the ASCEND pyramid looks like.

Within this framework, you will journey through a process of self-discovery that allows you to come into the awareness of where you are right now in your life and career. When was the last time you dedicated some time to yourself for reflection, connection, and to assess your current circumstances? I know I shouldn't have even asked, because I know the answer.

ASCEND METHOD

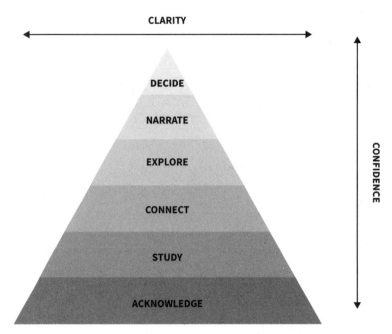

IMAGE BY: GALA JACKSON FOR INTERVIEWSNOB, LLC

Figure 4.2   The ASCEND pyramid

The society and culture that we live in today are, I believe, designed to keep us so busy that we run our lives on autopilot, accepting the status quo without critical thinking. Expecting that we will assimilate into a mindset and adopt the motto of "that's just the way it is and it's never going to change." Well, I'm a disruptor of the status quo especially when it comes to women and the way we work.

The ASCEND Practice

Next let's break down the ASCEND Practice piece by piece, then we'll get into exercises you can use for each step of the process.

- Acknowledge what is no longer working

    The first step in the ASCEND practice is to identify the core of your dissatisfaction and frustration with your job or career overall. This is often challenging to do because we are well acquainted with the symptoms of our dissatisfaction rather than the foundational issues. Ultimately, this is how we can keep landing in essentially the same job with the same type of manager just with a different company. *The goal with this part of the practice is awareness and identification – it will require courage.*

- Study your strengths

    As women we continuously overlook, minimize, and undervalue our strengths. Far too often, we don't even know what our strengths are and definitely don't know how to utilize and leverage them in a way that creates the success we desire. The key to success is not hustle; it's working smarter by leading with your strengths. *The goal of this part of the practice is to pinpoint what makes you unique.*

- Connect with your values

    Anytime we find ourselves in conflict or feel conflicted internally, it is because we are out of alignment with one or more of our values. Think about it. We know it happens in our personal lives with family and friends, but it also happens at work. Our values come into play with every communication transaction. When something isn't working at work – the difficult coworker, tough conversations with our boss, not connecting with the team, challenges as a people leader – there is a conflict of values.

    What's interesting is that we know our values in theory, but have difficulty articulating our values. Very rarely, if ever, do we share our values out loud or use them in a way that allows us to solve conflict at work or helps us to define professional success. Our values serve as our North Star, not only when it comes to personal decisions, but also when we are making decisions where we spend more than 50% of our time – at work. *The goal of this part of the practice is to identify, articulate, and use your values as a North Star as you define success and transition your career to reflect your values.*

- Explore your experiences

  When was the last time you sat down and reflected on your career from the very beginning until now? Better yet, took the time to consider the tasks within each of those roles to evaluate which tasks employed your strengths or put pressure on your weaknesses? Despite what you may be initially inclined to do, we are not going to be critical. We are going to celebrate. Every professional and personal experience you've had in your career is data that we can use to be successful. When we are seeking to transform our careers and achieve our own definition of success, we have to take the time to explore and evaluate our professional experiences – the good, the bad, and the ugly. All of it works together to serve our highest and greatest good. *The goal of this part of the practice is to recognize and celebrate all that you have done so far and use that information as clues to your pathway to success.*

- Narrate your story

  This step is where it gets real and can be an emotional part of the practice. Nurturing your voice requires that you *speak up.* So many women struggle in silence. And the most detrimental silence is when we are silent with ourselves. When we don't create space to say what we need and want, or tell the story of who we are. It matters that you know you are worthy and honor your voice, perspectives, and opinions in all spaces where you find yourself. The steps in this area include the importance of your voice on paper, within yourself, and out loud with others. *The goal of this part of the practice is to listen to your voice and value its power.*

- **Decide to embody the strongest, boldest, most courageous version of yourself**

    The culmination of each of the previous steps leads us to this final step of ASCEND where you'll practice embodying the strongest, boldest, most courageous version of yourself. Small steps and habits over each day and each week will add up quickly. You'll be surprised at how empowered, clear, and confident you will feel. The most important thing is that you won't just feel it, you'll know it too. Going through each step of the practice is ultimately designed to reintroduce yourself to yourself or maybe meet yourself, officially, for the very first time, if that makes sense. Holding space to acknowledge, reflect, evaluate, and explore your identity as a professional is the best course or certification you can ever take – period. *The goal of this part of the practice is to learn to undo things that no longer serve you, rewrite or eliminate false narratives that have been barriers to your success, and elevate the power of your own story to transform yourself and truly live out your definition of success.*

I am excited to walk though the next pages and chapters of this book with you. My excitement is fueled by doing this work with clients in real time and literally watching the transformation unfold. It is magical. It is necessary. It is healing. It is invigorating. I trust that you'll never be the same after doing this work. You'll understand how to confidently stand in every room that you find yourself in and know that you and your voice belong there.

I know the ASCEND method may sound intense, but I promise that each step is practical, realistic, and doable. There are actual prompts and exercises for you to do as often as it fits into your schedule. Whether it's something daily or you book a week-end retreat for yourself, we'll take each step, together, one step at a time.

Before we jump into each step of the practice, I encourage you to dedicate a journal specifically to this process, digital or paper. I also encourage you to consider doing this with another woman you know needs to experience this journey.

Want to share your thoughts with me?

 Join the conversation and download work-sheets from this chapter over on the Courage, Clarity, and Confidence website: www.courage clarityconfidence.com.

5

Acknowledge What Is No Longer Working

WHAT IS NO longer working for you?

It's a big question that needs a blank page ready for your candor. I didn't have a long list, but I had a list that felt heavy.

- I'm tired of working for a boss who doesn't get it.
- I'm tired of taking the brunt of my boss's inability to say no to more work.
- I'm done with feeling depleted at the end of my day.
- I do not want to manage people who constantly think they can do a better job than I can.

I bet one of those things triggered something in you. So let's do it – your turn! What's no longer working for you when it comes to work and how is it impacting your life outside of work? Be honest and real. Feel free to use the space here or grab your journal.

If we know something is no longer working, what keeps us in that particular place mentally or physically?

For me it was the golden handcuffs and my pride. I was frustrated but I was comfortable with the familiarity of the issues I was dealing with at work. The golden handcuffs were the praise for an achievement with a promotion on the horizon. And the salary didn't hurt either. My pride was steeped in the fact that I had grown an area of the business so quickly and effectively – it was a validation of my capabilities and expertise. I did not want anyone else to get credit for my hard work. There was no way I was going anywhere without my promotion and the bump in salary to go with it. The other piece was representation. Being a Black woman in a director level or above position is something that LESS than 4% of Black women hold. I wanted to be in a space where other women of color could see themselves and also contribute to increasing the number of Black women in leadership roles. Maybe I shouldn't call it pride, maybe it was noble, maybe both. But at the end of the day, I knew my time with the company had an expiration date. My workaholic behavior was at its peak and I know that behavior is a ticking time bomb. I had worked so hard to recover from being a workaholic and that one job unraveled it all. My health was sending me signs and signals that I had pushed too far. My relationships were becoming colder with one more "Can we reschedule?"

So what is it for you? What keeps you holding on when you know that something is no longer working and ultimately a detriment to you and your future? Use the following space to capture your thoughts.

Golden handcuffs are an incentive that is shiny and alluring. Usually offering financial rewards and security in exchange for something that you know is not what you ultimately want or need long term.

Source: Adapted from https://www.psychologytoday.com/au/blog/workplace-whisperers/201003/beware-the-golden-carrot-at-work

Dealing with Symptoms and Getting to the Truth

When we experience frustration in our life and career, we most often describe symptoms but rarely are we able to get to the root of the issues. I am definitely not a therapist, but as a coach it's important to explore the issues in such a way that you can identify the barrier, address it, and be able to move forward. The focus of our work in this book will be to name the symptoms, pinpoint the barrier, and devise a strategy to help you move forward.

In this first step, the goal is to identify the symptoms of what is no longer working. Some examples of symptoms include statements or phrases like:

- I don't like my boss
- My boss doesn't like me
- I hate going to work
- I feel undervalued and underappreciated at work
- I feel overwhelmed and burnt-out at work
- I want to quit this job
- Why am I not independently wealthy yet!? (This one is my personal favorite)

While these are all very valid and clear statements, they are symptoms of the situation – that is, these statements don't get underneath the surface to pinpoint that actual problem. I want you to take it a step further to grasp the core issue. You cannot effectively address what is not specifically identified. Table 5.1 shows some examples of questions you can pair with each of those aforementioned statements to help you drill down deeper.

As you answer the paired questions for further inquiry in the second column, you'll start to have revelation and insight into yourself. We often want to skip over the internal element: the underlying component that addresses the root. It's easier to address the symptoms and we typically think that changing jobs is the solution when it's just a temporary fix. We might land that new job and slightly higher pay, but the issues will resurface again. The next step is to consider what actions you can take to change or improve the circumstances. Feel free to use this template to pinpoint different symptoms, inquire, come into awareness, and consider action steps.

Table 5.1   Getting to the Root Exercise

Symptom:
- I don't like my boss

Inquiry:
- How do my and my boss's priorities differ?
- What value(s) are being violated by my boss?

Awareness + Revelation (as you inquire, what "aha" moments come up):

What can I do with this information now that I am aware of it?

Symptom:
- My boss doesn't like me

Inquiry:
- How would I describe my boss's personality?
- How is it similar or different from mine?
- How could those differences impact our work relationship?
- Why is it important to me that my boss likes me?

(continued)

Table 5.1 (Continued)

Awareness + Revelation (as you inquire, what "aha" moments come up):

What can I do with this information now that I am aware of it?

Symptom:
- I hate going to work

Inquiry:
- What about work feels stressful or causes anxiety for me?
- What about this job elicits feelings of hatred?

Awareness + Revelation (as you inquire, what "aha" moments come up):

What can I do with this information now that I am aware of it?

Table 5.1 (Continued)

Symptom:
• I feel undervalued and underappreciated at work

Inquiry:
• What additional tasks and responsibilities have I recently taken on?
• Where am I going above and beyond in my work? Who asked me to do more?

Awareness + Revelation (as you inquire, what "aha" moments come up):

What can I do with this information now that I am aware of it?

Symptom:
• I feel overwhelmed and burnt-out at work

Inquiry:
• What is it costing you to stay in an environment that leaves you feeling overwhelmed and burnt-out?
• What does a healthy work environment look like for you?
• What could ease and flow look like in your work?

Awareness + Revelation (as you inquire, what "aha" moments come up):

(continued)

Table 5.1 (Continued)

What can I do with this information now that I am aware of it?

Symptom:
- I feel overwhelmed and burnt-out at work

Inquiry:
- What is it costing you to stay in an environment that leaves you feeling overwhelmed and burnt-out?
- What does a healthy work environment look like for you?
- What could ease and flow look like in your work?

Awareness + Revelation (as you inquire, what "aha" moments come up):

What can I do with this information now that I am aware of it?

Learning to Honor My Value

Early in my career I learned this lesson. I was certain that the issues I was dealing with at work meant that it was time for me to leave. I had a boss who didn't get it. I was managing for the first time. I was tired of all of the after-hours work. Exhausted from all of the extroversion required to be successful in the job. After two years in the role, it was time for a change. I was clear on what I did not want to do in my next role. I wanted to be more behind the scenes, work a standard nine-to-five, and earn more. I did not want to manage professionals. Basically, I wanted to be a successful individual contributor and advance in my career as a successful individual contributor – almost unheard-of, right!? Although it's becoming more common in today's workforce. Regardless, that's what I wanted.

I applied for jobs and landed interviews quicker than I had expected. I was delighted and excited about the opportunities to choose from in my search. As I learned more about each role with each interview, there was a clear front-runner. An individual contributor role working with data and program development, not supervision or managment. The only outlier was the salary. Once I received the offer, I negotiated the best way I knew how at the time. They didn't budge, but the salary was around $5,000 more than I was earning at that time so I convinced myself to take it. The trade-off was being able to work a "desk job," go home at 5 p.m., and develop programs with colleagues, who I really enjoyed meeting during the interview process. I took the job and made plans to start after returning from a vacation.

The first few weeks in the role were great. I enjoyed the office environment, my colleagues, and learning about how my role and responsibilities fit into the larger landscape of really impactful work. But after those few weeks, I was asked to take on a very large initiative that required me to be a people leader. It was a stark change in job responsibilities. I literally cringed inside when I was asked. I can still feel those emotions, an indication of the severity of my inner turmoil.

Every ounce of my being said no, absolutely not. But what came out of my mouth were a few clarifying questions and a yes. I went back to my office and shut the door after that meeting. I cradled my forehead and literally said to myself, *this is why I quit my other job.* I took this particular job because it had no supervisory or management expectations, I could be behind the scenes, and have a traditional workday.

Whenever you work as a people leader, there is never a traditional workday and definitely not one that ends at 5 p.m. consistently, if ever. I even removed myself from an interview process from a very prominent organization with a higher salary to avoid having management responsibilities and nontraditional work hours. Managing large groups of people, always left me exhausted and overwhelmed. Working more than 8–9 hours a day burned me out completely. Don't get me wrong, I loved collaborating and leading people, but I needed to serve them in a way that honored my boundaries.

But WHY did I say yes when I clearly wanted and needed to say no? I hadn't dealt with the root issues of why I wanted, *needed*, in a new job. I dealt with the symptoms, but quickly found myself in the same environment and essentially helped to co-create it by not saying no.

Sound familiar?

When we find ourselves in situations like this, it's because we don't value ourselves enough. We are often unaware of our strengths and where we should best utilize our time and talent. When you understand your strengths and the value of them, you are careful when, where, and how you use them. So let's help you pinpoint your strengths so that when you find yourself with a proposition that deserves a no, you can say it with confidence, because you are choosing to honor yourself and your strengths.

Want to share your thoughts with me?

 Join the conversation and download worksheets from this chapter over on the Courage, Clarity, and Confidence website: www.courage clarityconfidence.com.

6

<u>S</u>tudy Your Strengths

I KNEW I shouldn't have accepted that job offer.

I was in Chicago exploring the city and stopped in a local boutique. I felt my phone ring and as I looked down I was thrilled to see the number pop up. I quickly stepped outside to take the call. I knew it would be the job offer I was waiting to receive.

The offer came with enthusiasm. But then we got to the salary and the thrill was gone. It was lower than what I promised myself I would accept. My heart sank and my anxiety was on the rise.

I was listening, but also thinking about how I was going to negotiate right then and there. I didn't want to waste time. To be honest, I didn't want that ache of anxiety and fear in the pit of my stomach for the rest of the night. I was on vacation and had already been through an intense job search process, my current job felt like the building was on fire, and this offer was the one that would determine whether I stayed in Atlanta or moved to Chicago. There were too many decisions that needed to be made and I felt that I couldn't afford to wait.

I mustered up all of the courage I had at the time and asked, "Is there any room to increase the salary?" Honestly, this is one of the worst ways to start a salary negotiation, asking a close-ended question, but you live and learn.

She said, "No." She explained that their offer was at the top of their range. I reiterated my excitement about the job, doubled down on the skills and experience I was bringing to the position, and I even explained that I would need more compensation to truly consider the role. I am sure she heard the disappointment and doubt in my voice. She wanted me to verbally accept during the call.

In an effort to get me to sign on, she made a commitment to personally help me get to the next level if I accepted the position. She was an executive leader. She was my boss's boss calling to make the offer, so I knew that they wanted me to take the job.

I paused.

I wasn't prepared for her to offer her personal support to help advance my career. It tugged at my vulnerability as a young, ambitious, woman who knew that she would need the support to get to the top. I respected her position for sure. I wanted to believe her. She seemed genuine. Yet still, the salary wasn't enough. But what I didn't have from any of my other job offers was the offer for help to get me to the next level.

I accepted the offer.

My concession was based on the "promise of potential" (that's what I refer to it as now). I decided to trust that she would invest in me and help me ascend in my career. One glaring problem that I didn't consider at that time was that we could have two totally different perspectives on when, how, and what getting to the "next level" could look like and become.

The "promise of potential," in my opinion, is exactly where many women's careers go to die – the promise of potential often offers no tangible pathway forward and absolutely nothing in writing. How do you include "maybe, someday soon" in an offer letter? I would venture to say that women receive more offers like this as compared to our male counterparts.

Within these "promise of potential" offers it's an invitation to get in and "prove yourself" in exchange for the support and help to advance. It's the birthplace of burnout.

If I had known then what I know now, I would never accept a job on the "promise of future career growth opportunities." I mean it sounds so nice, right? A glimmer of validation. A nod to our capability. The affirmation that someone sees potential in you. But I've never paid a single bill with potential. Learning from my own experience and that of my clients, I often find that taking a job opportunity laced with this type of possibility almost always leads to burnout, overwhelm, and some form of workplace trauma as a result.

These types of job offers are an invitation to prove our worth and value; something we already possess, which is why they want to hire us in the first place. Take note that the average job application receives 250 applications according to Zippia.[1] So you beat out on average 249 other candidates. You are their top choice, but they want to lowball you for your time, talent, and expertise. Never mind that on average women do not apply for a job until they meet 100% of the required skills and qualifications. The math ain't mathin' and I trust you are taking note of my point.

Our default in situations like this is often steeped in a scarcity mindset and that is the start of the slippery slope to burnout, overwhelm, and imposter syndrome. To demonstrate that we are "worthy" of the opportunity and potential opportunities, we turn ourselves inside out, moving out of alignment with ourselves and doubting what we thought was true about ourselves.

Scarcity Mindset: Limiting belief system rooted in fear that perceives life through the lens of limited options, opportunities, experiences.

Our natural inclination is to point the finger of blame and the employer is definitely a villain in this narrative, but not we do share in some of the responsibility, but not in the way you might think. We do actually value our skills, strengths, and experiences, but we've been taught that we should not value them in the same way a man values his skills, strengths, and experiences. We're brainwashed into believing the feminine leadership qualities we possess are of less value than masculine leadership qualities and that in order for us to advance in our careers we must dedicate our careers to acts of service and consistently prove loyalty and commitment to the work and/or the organization. It's hot trash.

We're just not confident – worn down by the many times we hear *no, not yet, close but not enough*. When we do finally receive an offer, it's a glimmer of hope. So we fold. Swallow that lump in our throat. Roll up our sleeves and get on the front lines of proving ourselves.

I wouldn't have been in that situation if I knew then what I know now – my strengths, their value, and the power of trust.

Discovering Your Strengths

After more than a decade of coaching clients, I've seen that my clients rave about learning about their strengths and how to leverage their natural skills and abilities to their advantage in any professional situation. The ability to identify and leverage your strengths to your advantage is a secret, powerful weapon.

We often become aware of our strengths after receiving words of external praise or celebration, or when we receive an accolade. We often need someone to call out our strengths because they are talents that are so natural or easy for us that we don't recognize they are not commonplace.

We spend so much time pursuing the perception of success, copying and comparing ourselves to others, that we overlook or even dismiss our own gifts and talents. No one can do what you do the way you do it. The world needs your specific fingerprints. Your specific perspective, style, and approach. And if you think we don't, take a trip to your local grocery store and consider all of the different brands of toilet tissue. Same job, so many different varieties, price points, and nuances that make every single brand different and desired by a specific type of customer. If the most basic things have strengths and unique qualities, you'd better believe you do too.

You might be wondering, How do I identify my strengths? You're probably realizing that you've been living from a place of survival. Doing what needs to be done or doing what you know without ever considering what you are uniquely gifted to do – and how that translates to a career you can enjoy. So much life has happened and continues to happen all around us that it feels almost impossible to take the time to investigate, explore, and pivot.

One of the tools I like to use often with clients is the Clifton-Strengths Assessment (most commonly known as the Strengths-Finder) by Gallup to help individuals pinpoint what makes them gifted. Normally, I am not a big fan of assessments. I find that most spit out a list of personality traits or characteristics too generically. But this particular assessment accounts for the qualities that make even two people who share the same "strength" unique. In fact, CliftonStrengths reports that the likelihood that you have the same strengths as others is 1 in 33 million. And that's just the strengths defined by the assessment, not how you personify those strengths at work or in your personal life, which can have more significant variations that make you one of a kind.

The assessment, developed by Dr. Donald O. Clifton, asks 177 questions to identify your strengths.[2] The assessment contains 34 strengths that fall into four core domains: Strategic Thinking; Execution; Influence; and Relationship Building. The CliftonStrengths Assessment seeks to pinpoint your natural inclination and approach to a variety of situations and instances to identify your strengths. Meaning that throughout the course of our lives our strengths remain fairly consistent. They'll shift occasionally depending on what major changes are happening in our lives, but we typically remain withing our top 10 strengths identified by the assessment. If you've never taken the Clifton-Strengths Assessment, I highly recommend that you do. And don't just stop at your results. Take the time to thoroughly read the Insights Guide that comes with your assessment results.

In case you are wondering, my Top 5 strengths are Futuristic, Strategic, Relator, Achiever, and Activator. What are yours? I would love for you to share your Top 5 with me. (Use the QR code at the end of this chapter.)

If you elect not to do the CliftonStrengths Assessment, there are alternatives to discovering your strengths. Seek out feedback from those you interact with on a regular basis and start asking some questions. You want to ask the following questions, and maybe a few of your own:

- What do you think I do better than anyone else that you know?
- What do you admire most about me?
- What can you always count on me to do no matter what?

And if asking others feels too daunting right now, here are some individual questions that you can reflect on to help you identify your strengths. I do encourage you to get feedback from at least one to two professionals whom you trust as supporting evidence and to ensure that you haven't left a strength behind.

- What work tasks energize you? How? Why?
- What can you do that feels so natural to you, you don't even realize you're doing it?
- What do you enjoy doing for others even when you are upset, stressed, or tired?
- If you were guaranteed the salary of your choice for the rest of your life, what work would you do?

Whether you do one or all three exercises, take some time to capture what you've learned about yourself and reflect on your findings. Do you notice any overlap or commonalities? Are there any particular themes that are emerging? Journal in the following space.

Now go back to your notes of reflection. Are there 3–5 or more strengths that you can identify? Once you have them identified, write them in the following space. Then take a moment to write out a "definition" of that strength. When and how does it show up? How would you explain it to someone you're meeting for the first time?

If you completed the CliftonStrengths Assessment, you'll want to read your Insights Guide and highlight or underline sentences and phrases that resonate with you the most and that illustrate your strengths in action. Once you have your sentences and phrases that resonate the most, consider how you would talk about each in your own words. Remember, the assessment helps you pinpoint your strengths and gives you a starting place for how you can describe and talk about your strengths. Feel free to modify or add to what you find in the report so that it's your voice describing your strengths. You even can print and cut out snippets from each section of your Insights Guide and add them in the following space, and capture some quick notes.

Capturing Your Strengths + Additional Space for Reflection

Strengths In Action

A client who often struggled with imposter syndrome and self-doubt in her professional capability enrolled in one of my six-week career bootcamps, where she learned about and took the CliftonStrengths Assessment for the first time. Skeptical at first because she had taken other assessments before and wasn't a fan of them, she was surprised that her results were so spot-on for her. After completing the bootcamp, the one thing that stood out to her the most was learning about her strengths.

We did a deep dive into her strengths, beyond just reviewing the results. We took each strength and explored how it showed up in her day-to-day work life, how she could become more aware of her strengths in action, and how she could leverage her strengths in challenging situations at work and for career advancement. We even discussed how she could use them with her annual goals and performance review. We also discussed considering the possible strengths of her colleagues and how she could use that knowledge to enhance work relationships and work flows.

She went from struggling to clearly articulate her value and unique skill set to knowing her value proposition. As part of the bootcamp course she had to draft a value proposition statement. She wrestled with it a bit. She struggled with talking about herself so positively. She realized she had been underestimating herself for far too long.

After the session she shared with me and the rest of the participants, "Going through this work, no one can ever tell me what I'm not. People can form a lot of opinions about me, but one thing they can't do is tell me what I am not."

It was a huge breakthrough for her not just professionally, but personally too. She evolved from a doubtful professional, despite her years of incredible experience, to a confident expert in her field, ready to secure business deals and advance in her career. She went on to close a six-figure deal in her own business shortly after our work together.

She was able to experience this transformation because she didn't stop at being able to identify her strengths; she learned how to articulate and leverage those strengths. She had clarity on how she showed up in rooms and was prepared to navigate in any situation she found herself in professionally, or personally, because she was clear on her assets and their value.

I AM . . . Strengths Statements Exercise

Once you have identified, explored, and studied your strengths, I want you to engage in a transformative exercise that will affirm your strengths while also offering phenomenal talking points to include in a value proposition statement or an interview. The exercise is called *I am . . . Strengths Statements.* In this activity, you list and define your strengths and provide examples of how your strengths are demonstrated in a professional environment, then construct an affirmative "I am . . ." statement to illustrate the value of your strength.

Here is an example of how to complete this exercise:

Strength #1: Relator

Definition: You occasionally uncover how and why things happen as they do

Example #1 of this strength in action in a work environment: Ask open-ended questions

Example #2 of this strength in action in a work environment: Listening for patterns, trends, and clues; gathering feedback from colleagues and interpreting that feedback against the challenge or problem that needs to be solved

Because of this strength, I can: I help my colleagues pinpoint the root cause or bottleneck of a problem.

"I AM" statement: I am a problem solver who collects relevant data points by asking open-ended questions while listening for patterns, trends, and clues. By asking the appropriate questions I am able to develop solutions that can resolve business challenges.

Strength #1
Definition:

Example #1 of this strength in action in a work environment:

Example #2 of this strength in action in a work environment:

Because of this strength, I can help my employer, colleagues, companies:

I AM statement:

Strength #2
Definition:

Example #1 of this strength in action in a work environment:

Example #2 of this strength in action in a work environment:

Because of this strength, I can help my employer, colleagues, companies:

I AM statement:

Strength #3
Definition:

Example #1 of this strength in action in a work environment:

Example #2 of this strength in action in a work environment:

Because of this strength, I can help my employer, colleagues, companies:

I AM statement:

Strength #4
Definition:

Example #1 of this strength in action in a work environment:

Example #2 of this strength in action in a work environment:

Because of this strength, I can help my employer, colleagues, companies:

I AM statement:

Strength #5
Definition:

Example #1 of this strength in action in a work environment:

Example #2 of this strength in action in a work environment:

Because of this strength, I can help my employer, colleagues, companies:

I AM statement:

Once you have all of your I AM statements complete, consider how you can utilize those sentences to build a branding statement. A brand statement is similar to a value proposition statement. It is a carefully curated statement that informs current and potential employers of the problems you can solve as well as your capability, skills, experience, and value-add to the company.

Here is an example of a branding statement, built through this exercise:

Accounts Receivable professional seeking to resolve organizational challenges efficiently. Active contributor with the ability to lead tasks and projects independently or with teams that possess a high achievement orientation. Seeks a detailed understanding of objectives to consistently deliver comprehensive results with zero excuses. Proficient at meeting deadlines with tight timelines in high pressure situations. Self-starter who thrives in environments with open dialogue, clear expectations, and goals.

Now I'll walk you through how to create your own.

List all of your I AM Statements below:

Next, prioritize each statement in order of importance or relevance to your current or desired role:

Now, put your prioritized sentences into a paragraph (start with a quick rough draft, you can always edit later):

Anything missing that you want to include? Jot it down below.
Ideas:

- Industry
- Title
- Years of Experience

Now write a more polished version of your rough draft adding
any additional information you felt was missing:

Bravo!
What do you think about your statement?

Want to share your thoughts with me?

Join the conversation and download worksheets from this chapter over on the Courage,
Clarity, and Confidence website: www.courage
clarityconfidence.com.

7

Connect with Your Values

LEARNING TO IDENTIFY and beginning to listen to your own voice reveals your values. Knowing your values, but more importantly, being able to articulate how your values impact your life and work, is critical for career fulfillment and success. One thing I have personally learned and observed through work with my clients is that all conflict – interpersonal and intrapersonal – is a result of values being violated. Being able to honor your own values and respect others' values will be the solution to almost every conflict.

First, let's quickly establish a universal definition of what values are. Values are the principles or ideas that govern a person's character, actions, decisions, and communication style. Values are what is most important to us and what we appreciate in others. I like to think of it like this: values are our drivers. The standards by which we live and evaluate others. They are why we do what we do.

We typically two sets of values, personal and professional. As we start this particular chapter, I am going to ask you to consider

79

what your values might be, and then identify and define them from a personal perspective, and finally from a professional perspective. Moving through this chapter, we'll discuss why our values are such a critical piece of alignment and success. Your values serve as your North Star in your career evolution and progression. Let's jump right in!

When you think about values in your life, what might some of your values be personally? What values guide your actions and decisions? What values are present in your relationships with close family, friends, or new acquaintances?

Identifying Your Personal Values

Make a list here (aim for 3–5 values):
Value #1:

Value #2:

Value #3:

Value #4:

Value #5:

Next, define what those values mean to you in your own words:

Value #1:

Value #2:

Value #3:

Value #4:

Value #5:

Struggling to make your list? Here are some examples to help you get started:

Security	Balance
Trust	Family
Loyalty	Growth
Optimism	Innovation
Achievement	Collaboration
Compassion	Integrity
Environment	Transparent communication
Responsibility	Service to others
Fairness	Open-mindedness
Adventure	Ethics
Appreciation	Honesty
Curiosity	

Now let's think about your career and the way you work. What values are important to you professionally? Are they honesty, compassionate leadership, transparent communication or other things?

As you create your list of professional values, you may notice that there is overlap between what you identify for your personal values and your professional values. The overlap is to be expected and it's OK to duplicate values as needed. As a point of consideration, note whether your definition of the value shifts between your personal life and professional life. For example, appreciation might be a value for you in both your personal and professional life, but how you define appreciation and want to be appreciated may be different in your personal life than it is in your professional world.

Identifying Your Professional Values

Make a list here (aim for 3–5 values):

Value #1:

Value #2:

Value #3:

Value #4:

Value #5:

Define what those values mean to you in your own words:

Value #1:

Value #2:

Value #3:

Value #4:

Value #5:

Now that you have your two lists, what do you notice? Where are there similarities and where are there differences?

Still feeling a bit stuck? Following are some sentence prompts that might help you pinpoint your personal or professional values:

- The things that make me feel seen, heard, understood, or calm have to do with the presence of *this value:*

- The things that make me feel stressed, frustrated,, or feel afraid, have to do with the absence of *this value:*

- Whenever I made major changes, I was motivated by *this value:*

- When I think about experiences in the past that have left me feeling a sense of regret or disappointment, it's most likely because *I did not honor this value:*

If you had a difficult time identifying your values and would like more support, there is a free assessment online at VIACharacter.org to help get you started. The VIA assessment refers to values as character strengths. Once you have your assessment results, print out your results and add to or modify the results. Values are unique to you! It's also a good idea to keep that print out in a place where you can reference it as needed.

Values as a North Star

With every single position I've held and every career transition I've navigated, I can look back on each and see how my values impacted every decision I made or decision I wish I had made. I've learned that my values are an anchor in the rough seas of uncertainty and a calm in the midst of a storm of transition and change. They have been and continue to be a light to help me navigate through the darkness and I hope they'll become that for you too.

I was first invited to consider my values while reading a book called *Chazown: Discover and Pursue God's Purpose for Your Life.* It was early in my career when I was struggling to find meaning and myself all those nights that I sat on the couch berating myself for not being more grateful back in chapter 3.

In the book, author Craig Groeschel invites you to identify your core values as part of his framework for circling the truth to find your purpose.[1] It was the first time anyone had ever asked me, "What makes me angry with a righteous anger?" And, "What do I absolutely love, more than anything else?" Simple, but powerful questions. They were questions I didn't know I needed.

The purpose of these questions was to help me, the reader, pinpoint what mattered most to me. At the end of the day or at the end of my life, what core values would I have lived by? Those core values would guide me through the unknowns of my life and career. The would-be cords of my legacy weaving throughout my story. I wrestled with the process of identifying my values. It seemed daunting at first to find the words that were comprehensive enough to capture my beliefs, but when I took the time to see what was already there – meaning that I was giving myself a permission slip to stay what was most important to me independent of what others thought my values "should be" – it was much easier to make a list. After a few iterations of the list, I had my five values. While those values have evolved with me over the years, knowing my values has served as a constant North Star in my life, especially when it comes to career decisions.

Our careers are where we spend the most of our time. If we were to segment our lives, our careers would most likely be the biggest portion. It matters that we honor our values in our career. Just as important as the parallel of our personal everyday lives. Honoring my values, while not the easiest or most convenient, has not led me to a place of regret. In fact, not operating in alignment with my values has almost always led me to a place of regret.

If you find yourself with an opportunity to leave an organization that is not in alignment with your values and can do so quickly, do it. You'll be glad you did and better off for it. But if you have other factors that may prevent you from leaving immediately, use your values to create a strategic plan for your exit. I rarely ever advise people to just quit their job without thoughtful consideration, but when it comes to neglecting your values I am always going to advocate that you follow your values before you follow anything else.

Likewise, if you find a career path and job opportunity that allows you honor your values, go for it! Each time you move in alignment with your values, you gain clarity and confidence.

As you think about where you've been in your career and where you are now, how have you moved in alignment with your values? How have you operated against or ignored your values? What were the outcomes? Compare the two. Use the space below to capture your thoughts. I'll bet that you don't regret moving in alignment with your values. I'll also bet you won't regret it in the future either.

Want to share your thoughts with me?

 Join the conversation and download worksheets from this chapter over on the Courage, Clarity, and Confidence website: www.courage clarityconfidence.com.

8

Explore Your Professional Experiences

I WAS RECENTLY working with a client who was dealing with self-doubt and worried about finding a new job. This is a common issue.

She said, "Every time I look at job boards I see all of these jobs, but nothing that seems to truly be a fit. In the rare instance that I do find something I think is a fit, I apply, and then hear nothing back. And I have no idea if I am even targeting the right positions or if the compensation will be what I need. It's clear that I don't know what I am doing or if my résumé is the problem because I am not getting any calls. I don't know what to do! No one wants to give me a chance."

Sound familiar?

She didn't want to be looking for another job in the first place, but couldn't put up with the blatant disrespect and undermining at work. Not to mention she just found out that her male counterpart was making $20,000 more for the exact same job with less experience, and he was causing bottlenecks for multiple teams.

She was up for a promotion and heard, "Not yet" again. She was fed up and rightfully so.

Similar experience?

I'm not surprised. You are not alone. In fact, you're in good company. I hear stories like this all too often.

As my client was talking, I could hear a clear undertone. She felt like she was the problem. Not knowing what to do, how to do it, her résumé, etc. The frustration was consuming her and she was near tears. Hear me right here: *It is not your fault.*

We struggle in job search because what we've been taught in terms of getting a job is outdated. In fact, the moment we start looking at job boards and searching for specific titles, we are in trouble. Not to mention the traditional job search process sorely underserves women and people of color.

I responded to my client, "Let's talk more about this and dig deeper. It sounds like we need to put your search in perspective. Here are some things you may not realize . . .

"First, all available jobs are not posted on job boards or online at all.

"Second, you're only getting a snapshot of jobs at a particular window of time and based on job titles that are ambiguous and without continuity across industries, company size, or company type.

"Third, submitting your application online alone is not enough. Companies often give priority to candidates who have a referral or internal connection to the company. Prioritizing connections and conversations over application submissions is key.

"Fourth, do you realize how talented and valuable you are to an employer? Have you considered that you need a strategic career plan and a clear value proposition that brings job opportunities to you?"

My fourth point stirred up something in her. It was designed to do so.

She asked, "What do you mean? How can I bring job opportunities to myself?"

I said, "Clarity is a magnet."

The Traditional Job Search Underserves Women

The Latin word for clarity is *claritas*, which means "glory, divine splendor."[1] I firmly believe that when you are able to clearly pinpoint your value, it puts you in direct alignment with the boldest, strongest, and most courageous version of yourself. When you are in that mindset and presence, everything that is destined for you starts to move toward you and materialize in your life. It's akin to the laws of attraction.

Now, let's take that revelation and go back to the concept of the traditional job search, which typically includes the following steps:

1. Search ambiguous job titles and job descriptions.
2. Write a résumé. Debate between three or four pages of everything you've done in your career, or cram it all into one page.
3. Stress out about applicant tracking systems (ATS) and algorithms.
4. Apply for a job online. Meticulously fill in all the blanks the system said it would do for you if you uploaded your résumé.
5. Manage the frustration and exhaustion of ONE application, then psyche yourself up for another one.
6. Blindly compete with hundreds of other applicants (the average job posting receives 250 applications).
7. Anxiously wait for a call or email and pray you don't miss it.

Old.

Antiquated.

Out of touch.

And a guaranteed way to catapult yourself into self-doubt, second-guessing, and worry. Also, a really high probability that you'll wind up in a job you don't really want, but you'll likely take it just to end the frustration of the job search process.

And as if working in a job you don't truly want wasn't enough, I would venture to say that women in particular lose the most compensation, hindering overall earning potential, if they land the job via an online application alone. I have not had a client land their dream job via an online application alone. It's just not been my experience over the last decade.

The cycle is perpetual throughout your career unless you take ownership of your career, unabashedly recognize the value of your experience and skills, and understand that employees are the real MVPs of any company.

As we continue the work of gaining clarity and coming into the awareness and acknowledgment of who we are, we have to talk about the experience that we have garnered through our careers, both the personal and professional lessons learned that have shaped who we are as talented professionals. Just as we did with our values and our strengths, we want to spend some time pinpointing key experiences that were defining moments for us as professionals. The moments that sharpened our business acumen, made us better leaders, established our workstyle. And those experiences can be both positive and negative. They all culminate in learning, development, and growth. Sometimes our most challenging moments are our greatest teachers. And the most fun and enjoyable experiences can teach us just as much. We want to take advantage of both experiences as we inventory your experience and the skills that you've cultivated throughout your career to date.

I want you to take a moment to look at your résumé or your LinkedIn profile. whichever one has the most comprehensive information about your career path today. I invite you to ask yourself a series of questions regarding your experience.

As you look back over the roles that you've held throughout your career, consider the following questions below but wait to answer later, using the chart at the end of this chapter.

I encourage you to wait until the of this chapter to answer these questions because you'll want ample time for reflection and evaluation. Reading the rest of this chapter beforehand will also help you better understand the purpose of each question. However, if you do see one question below that causes an immediate reaction, take a moment to jot down what comes up in the margin next to it, then dive deeper with the chart at the end of the chapter.

12 Questions To Help You Inventory Your Career Experience

1. What experiences or roles did you enjoyed the most? Why?
2. What did you specifically enjoy about each role? Which particular tasks?
3. What experiences or roles did you not enjoy? Why?
4. What did you specifically not enjoy about each role? Which particular tasks?
5. What could you see yourself doing in the future?
6. What work or tasks energized you and felt as though they came naturally to you?
7. What work or tasks depleted you and made you feel like you had to overextend yourself to complete?
8. What would you never want to do again?
9. What problems are you able to solve?

10. What problems do you want to solve?

11. In what ways have you added impact or value? How do you want to add impact and value as you move forward in your career?

12. What would you jump at the opportunity to do again?

Just Because You Can, Doesn't Mean You Should

Note that just because you can do something does not mean that you want to do it. Consider that distinction. Oftentimes we fall into the habit of doing things simply because we *can* or because everyone thinks we're good at it, but it's not something we actually enjoy, want to do, or feel confident doing.

I'll use myself as an example:

I started my career in the coaching industry as a résumé writer. I can write a really fantastic résumé but I do not enjoy writing résumés anymore. I don't find fulfillment in using my skills and experience in that way. I don't believe it to be the greatest area in which I can make an impact. What I do believe is my career arc is coaching women as they navigate a career transition. In particular, I know that my strengths as an active listener, strategic thinker, futurist, empath, and activator make me a phenomenal coach for the woman who is ready to transition and show up in her career differently – as the boldest and strongest version of herself.

Making the transition out of résumé writing was hard for me. I built a business and brand around writing résumés. Clients struggled to understand why I was no longer writing résumés, referrals kept coming in for résumés, but I was committed to the pivot. I had inventoried my experience and skills, determining that I could make a bigger impact as a coach. I'm so glad I made the switch! It's opened up doors of abundance for me, including this book that you're holding in your hands right now.

When I hear clients tell me that they do a lot of work simply because it needs to be done, no one else will do it, and they can do it, I CRINGE. I know the real reason they do it is because we make the mistake of thinking that doing more translates to promotion. It's important for me to acknowledge that part of what we deal with at work has to do with the fact that we are *assigned* gender normative tasks outside of the scope of our actual job duties. Things like taking notes, scheduling, and other administrative tasks deemed more "suitable" for a woman to do. In these instances, you have to call it out and push back, advocating for yourself and the women who will come alongside or after you.

As for doing more work because we think it will lead to a promotion, if you haven't learned just yet, that is a *gigantic* lie. The truth is doing less and *being* is the pathway to success. It's not doing more and it's definitely not making yourself synonymous with tasks or work you do. Instead, we should focus on who we are, becoming the best version of ourselves while doing work we are uniquely gifted to do and are most interested in doing. Then we proactively seek out opportunities that allow us to be appreciated and valued for who we are and the work we are gifted to do.

I know it sounds like I'm living in la-la land, but it's reality. It can be your reality too. It is absolutely against the status quo and takes a lot of courage and clarity to do it, but breaking the "rules" is how you win the game.

As you review and evaluate each of your previous roles to date in your career, there are questions in the chart below that will help you pinpoint what energized you and what drained you.

Acknowledge all of the things that you can do. Then consider out of all of the things you *can* do, what do you *want* to do? Think about what energizes you. Think about what is worthy of your energy, your capacity, and your time.

If you want to take this a step further and dive deep after considering what you want to do and the things that energize you, ask yourself how do I do those tasks or work in a way that no one else does or can? What is my unique perspective, vantage point, or method?

Doing this deeper dive will require mental and emotional space. I encourage you to change your physical location if you can or go get out in nature. "Our physiological, psychological, and emotional states change as our surroundings change. Natural places relax us. We're able to focus better and we feel more emotionally engaged."[2]

There's physical space for you to dive deep at the end of this chapter. Go for it!

What's Next?

Once you've reflected on, inventoried, and evaluated your professional experience and skills throughout your career, start to consider how the dots connect with your values and strengths. Using each step of the ASCEND method – we have two more key areas to go through – we are going to pinpoint your career arc. Your *career arc* is the peak on which a thriving, successful career and life resides. It allows you to move in alignment and make the biggest impact, while consistently honoring who you are as a woman and a professional.

Your career arc will serve as a guiding light, providing direction as you navigate every aspect of your career journey. Utilizing your career arc is how you'll be able to create a life of freedom and abundance, professionally and personally. This is also how you'll begin to redefine success in your career. You'll focus on all that you are, the who – identify the problems you want to solve, the what – and recognize what you are uniquely positioned to do – the how.

I recognize that it can be challenging for women in particular to identify their career arc. I recognize that it's difficult to discover what you can do that no one else can do the way that you do. We are so used to doing everything for everyone all the time, putting ourselves last, and we are rarely have the opportunity to sit down and evaluate what it is that we want to do. To ask ourselves what is it that makes me come alive? What work do I enjoy? What life do I want to live? We have to say no more often in order to say yes to what matter most. The ability to say no starts with the knowledge of who you are and what is in alignment with the vision you have of yourself.

I also recognize that the opportunity to even do this work can appear to come from a place of privilege. Not all women have the opportunity to take the time to identify what it is that they choose to do versus what it is that they have to do to survive or meet the needs around them. But I want to respectfully submit to you that it does not have to be a place of privilege. If you're seeking to level up and advance and grow, to live in a place of abundance, this work is absolutely necessary, and there will be a season or opportunity to do this work. Finding or making the time to pause, evaluate, and decide how you will show up is critical. It's a daily decision. In this work, as you may have already noticed, I'm asking you to explore and understand the key components of who you are that will be drivers for your success, however you choose to define it.

Fulfillment and joy lie within how you utilize your strengths, honor your values, leverage your experience, use your voice, and eliminate what is no longer serving you so you can courageously and confidently embody the boldness of who you are and live your life on purpose.

A Note About the Exercise Ahead

Sitting down and trying to do this exercise myself when I was in my own season of discovery and transformation, trying to identify my experiences and my skills, I really struggled to figure out what was unique to me or what I saw as valuable.

Oftentimes what comes to us naturally and what we enjoy is not viewed as work. That makes this exercise really difficult – to see what your unique gifts are in terms of skills and experiences. You may need to rely on some of the feedback from individuals who know you well, colleagues, supervisees, and supervisors who can give you feedback on what you do really well, things that others don't do the way that you do. Keep in mind that just because it is easy for you doesn't mean it's less valuable; in fact it is more valuable. Believe it or not, the adage is true, work doesn't have to feel like work to be work. Work can be and needs to have ease and flow to be sustainable and truly integrate into our lives.

Some of the questions that you may find yourself wanting to ask your close network are: What is it that I do that no one else can do? How have you seen me in action? What type of work or tasks do I get excited about doing? Where have you seen my magic show up? In addition to inventorying your skills and experiences on your own, having this external feedback can help you zero in on the things that can be more challenging for us to see for ourselves.

Exercise: 12 Questions to Help You Inventory Your Career Experience

What experiences or roles did you enjoy the most? Why?	

What did you specifically enjoy about each role? Which particular tasks?	
What experiences or roles did you not enjoy? Why?	
What did you specifically not enjoy about each role? Which particular tasks?	
What work or tasks energized you and felt as though they came naturally to you?	
What work or tasks depleted you and felt like you had to overextend yourself to complete?	

What problems are you able to solve? What problems do you want to solve?	
In what ways have you added impact or value in your career?	
What would you never want to do again?	
What would you jump at the opportunity to do again?	
As you consider your answers, does anything stand out to you as a pattern or recurring theme? What do you notice?	

A Deeper Dive

What do I now know about myself that I didn't know before this exercise?

What is my unique perspective, vantage point, or method to the work that energizes me?

Want to share your thoughts with me?

 Join the conversation and download worksheets from this chapter over on the Courage, Clarity, and Confidence website: www.courage clarityconfidence.com.

9

<u>N</u>arrate Your Story

In 2014, I had the opportunity to deliver my first TED Talk at TEDx Kennesaw State University entitled "The Power of Story." A quick internet search will bring it right up if you want to check it out. I stepped onto the stage, stood in the center of that famous red dot, and told the story about my career pivot and transition into entrepreneurship for the first time.

I didn't quite know it at the time, but my story became the blueprint for the work I do today. Personally navigating some of the steps in the ASCEND practice when I was lost and seeking career (and life) clarity – then standing on that stage – was a full circle moment. Connecting with our own stories and becoming the hero in our own storyline, I believe, becomes the map to fulfilling our life's purpose and mission. It was and continues to be true for me. My story all culminated in the ASCEND practice, became the catalyst for stepping into entrepreneurship, and now this book. I didn't know that while going through it in real time, but I'm glad I didn't quit. What was a pivotal moment for me – using my voice to tell my story on such a grand stage – gave birth to this next piece of the practice, the power and importance of narrating your own story.

As women, it is critical that we find our voice and tell our own story, right down to our career. If you don't tell the story of who you are, someone else will make assumptions and tell a story for you. And we know there are FAR too many false narratives and stories about us. It's because men have been trying to tell our stories for us for *DECADES*. But not anymore. We do not have to have our individual and collective stories to be dictated to us by an incompetent manager, nor be defined by one career valley, one career peak, or a few lines on a résumé. We can and must tell our own comprehensive story that demonstrates resilience, value, capability, and achievement. We need to be clear on the problems that we are uniquely qualified to solve and align our careers accordingly. Working for companies that value women employees and have workplace policies and cultures that reinforce the commitment to wellness at work. It requires that we speak up and use our voices and stop taking no for an answer.

Standing on that infamous red dot, the spotlight was literally blinding, and I was terrified. Mostly because of the pressure – I mean it's TED Talk! But more so because I was telling my story of transformation. I wasn't sure if it would resonate well or if I would mess up or forget something (recording it is a one-shot deal and there is a live audience). But the main cause of my fear was that I realized at that moment how my voice had been used in service and support of others, but very rarely ever used to tell my story. Not surprising. I somehow, unconsciously at the time, believed that telling my story was boastful even though it was true. It was the story of my career pivot – a firsthand account. I was using my voice to share something personal and vulnerable out loud to complete strangers and have it recorded for the rest of the world to see. I'll never forget what it was like for me to tell my own story, about me, courageously. In my own words, and with my own voice. I gave myself a permission slip to abandon the "shoulds" and the fear to stand authentically as myself and trust that it would be enough.

During my talk I shared how powerful stories are, particularly our own personal narratives. I talked about how our brains are hardwired for stories. Stories are information. They help us make sense of the world around us and help us to draw conclusions. To complete their evaluation, our brains require a beginning, middle, and an end of a story. When we're missing one of the critical pieces of a story – the beginning, middle, or end – our brain seeks to fill in the gap for us. Right, wrong, or indifferent. It doesn't evaluate the piece that is missing as fact or fiction, it just needs the data to assess safety or danger – that's it. And our brains do this as a means to protect us, ultimately. To assess and evaluate if there's any imminent fear or danger that we should consider and react accordingly.

Stories are how our brains like to naturally process information. Think about it; stories are *everywhere*. Songs, television, books, podcasts, social media, résumés, and our careers. And there are so many stories that we carry around with us, so many good stories that encourage us and motivate us and keep us going. Then there are stories that are challenging and hard for us to experience and tell. There are stories about us, with us, and sometimes for us.

When we consider how our brains process information and factor in the context of our careers, the topic gets expansive. Stories extend to our reputation and brand. They precede us before walking into a room.

What is your story?

What do you want your story to become?

These two questions are rhetorical for now, but as we move forward in this chapter, we are going to explore your story and what you want your story to become. Before you can tell your own story, you have to acknowledge any narratives that are not your own.

Understanding Your Own Story

In order to tell your story, you have to address the barriers that hinder your belief in your worth and voice. Ironically, these barriers are stories or a single story that keeps you stuck. Typically, there is one single story that runs as the underlying current or root story. I refer to it as the core limiting belief. There can be multiple stories, but usually they all reinforce the same root narrative.

We want to find out what that root story is so we can address your core limiting belief. To do that I have one question for you to consider:

What stories are at play in your life right now?

As you explore this primary question, I want you to consider the following secondary questions to help you capture the commonalities across multiple stories that could be a play in your life right now:

- What stories are you telling yourself?
  Example: I'm not good enough.
- What stories are people intentionally or unintentionally telling you about yourself or situation?
  Example: You don't have what it takes to be a leader.
- What stories from your past, personal or professional, are you carrying around as if they were your own, but they really belong to someone else?
  Example: You can never trust people.
- What if any common themes do you notice?

BIG. GIGANTIC. QUESTIONS.

I know, I know . . . I should have warned you. It's like a moment where something just stops you immediately in your tracks. Use the following space to reflect on and start answering these questions. As you continue with this chapter, feel free to come back and revisit these questions and add to them.

What stories are you telling yourself?

What stories are people intentionally or unintentionally telling you about yourself or situation?

What stories from your past, personal or professional, are you carrying around as if they were your own, but they really belong to someone else?

What if any common themes do you notice?

Taking the time to consider and answer these questions is a critical part of uncovering your story and reconnecting with your voice. In order to elevate in any capacity, you have to remove the barriers and weights that keep you stuck living in a lower level of existence. The barrier is often something someone said about you that stung and then stuck. That narrative became the birth-place of the struggle with doubt, lack of confidence, insecurity, and acceptance. It's caused you to play small and withdraw from the fullness of who you are, undervaluing the talent and skills that you possess. You have to identify the negative narratives, replace them with the truth, and take ownership of your story.

Take some time to journal and reflect. You can answer these questions through a personal and professional lens. As mentioned earlier, we can't talk about the professional without talking about the personal.

To give you some context, if you were to lay these questions within the context of your career, there may be single-story narratives with components that sound like this:

I need another certificate or degree before I'll qualified.

I need more experience.

I don't know enough.

I'm not the right fit.

I'm too emotional.

I'm stuck in this career.

I don't know how to lead.

I'll never get promoted.

I'm not a good communicator or presenter.

They just don't like me.

There are no jobs.

I'm not good at this.

I'm too old.

I'm too young.

Do any of those stories sound familiar to you?

What other stories are there that exist for you?

These narratives can come from other people, but they can also be things that you say about yourself to yourself. Typically, such stories are the result of a criticism you received from someone else, but they can also be internal, a mistake you made that you can't forgive yourself for just yet. An embarrassing moment that feels just as real as the day it happened so long ago. A single snapshot in time that replays far too often. But what matters right now is identifying the story that you're telling yourself right now in this season of your life and then dealing with how that narrative is impacting you.

We are often governed by our *feelings*. They can become dictators in our life if we're not aware and intentionally seek to address those feelings with facts. If left unaddressed, those stories we're carrying around can create triggers that cause an extreme reaction every time it comes up – or become stumbling blocks that cause more damage.

You have to replace the old narrative with a new one.

Identifying Your Own Voice

There's so much noise that keeps us from seeing ourselves clearly. Society, culture, bias, and more. And one of the things that you'll have to do in the process of identifying where you are is to get quiet and listen. And that quiet may mean going away for a weekend, taking a full day off for yourself, taking half a day or simply an hour, if that's all that you can do. But spending time getting quiet and discerning what is your internal voice and what is the voice of an external entity is necessary.

What does your voice sound like?

How do you talk to yourself? Are you critical or compassionate?

What other voices do you hear? Who do they belong to?

Is it your mother? Father?

Brother or sister?

A former friend?

Partner?

Boss?

Mentor?

Identify that voice.

You know that voice . . . the one when you are preparing for an interview, getting ready for the first day on your new job, or reviewing notes for an important presentation at work. Yes, that one.

The voice that says,

"Oh, you're about to embarrass yourself again?"

"They're going to know you're a fake."

"You can't do this – you know what happened last time."

It makes me sick to my stomach – the way we allow those voices to take up so much mental, emotional, and physical space in our lives.

Let's investigate that voice and replace it with your voice and your truth.

What was the context of that situation in which those words were spoken? What is no longer true about who you are right now versus who you were then? Consider whether those negative words were ever even true. Right now, spend some time thinking about how that voice shows up for your present day and consider how it is impacting your career growth and trajectory.

If that narrative is no longer true, then what is true now? What is different? What has changed? The truth can be as simple as, "I have grown, I'm not the same person I was. I've had more experiences."

Let's set the record straight. Use the exercise below, Identify the Messenger to identify the messenger and pinpoint what is true today.

And if you don't believe that you have a truth to put in that negative narrative yet, consider what you *want* to be true about that narrative. What do you want to say in response to it? What do you know about your capability and ability that you can use to replace that false negative narrative, even if it's the future you're referencing?

The thing that I love about stories is that they do in fact have a beginning, a middle, and an end. And with these negative narratives, it's just the beginning or middle of the story. But it is never at the end. The end of the narrative *always* belongs to you. And that is the incredible thing about your story: it can always evolve and you can change it going forward at any time.

Exercise #1: Identifying the Messenger

What voice or narrative starts talking when you seek to do something new or something that you want to do for yourself?

What is that message?

Whose voice does that message belong to?

And where were you when you first heard this negative voice that stuck with you?

What do you attempt to do or actually do when that voice appears?

What was the context of that situation in which those words were spoken?

What is no longer true about who you are right now versus who you were then?

Were those negative words ever even true?

If that narrative is no longer true, about who you were, then we're about your ability or capability and what you know to be true. What is the truth now?

And if you don't believe that you have a truth to put in that negative, false narrative yet, what do you want to be true about that narrative?

What do you want to say in response to it?

What do you know about your capability and ability that you can replace that false negative narrative with even if it's the future you're referencing?

I want to take this moment to let you know that I am so proud of you! Even through the pages of this book, I see YOU. You are a gift and a treasure to this world. I cannot wait to see how you show up as the strongest, boldest, most courageous version of yourself full of courage, clarity, and confidence. We, the collective of women, need you, your voice, and all that you have to offer as we change the world for the greater good. Brava!

How to Change the Narrative

An exercise I learned to facilitate while working with one of my clients helped to uncover the difference between her voice and those of others. Just as important, it helped her release the narrative from that external party and allowed her to replace that narrative with a new one – the truth of who she was now.

During our coaching relationship, she shared that she felt stuck in her career. She was overwhelmed by work and feeling burnt out. During a coaching session, we identified her strengths, explored her values, and discussed her experience. We navigated pros and cons of the career pivot, and the pros outweighed the cons. She desperately wanted to change, but just couldn't make the shift into pursuing what she identified as her calling and passion. She was clear about what she needed to do, but just could not follow through. There was a lot of hesitation around a change that was fairly low risk with high reward.

We leaned into curiosity and explored what the hesitation could be. Through a series of questions, she shared that she had a fear of failure. The fear of failure stemmed from her childhood. In her childhood she learned not to take risks. She learned that criticism came along with failure. The criticism came from her mother. Every time she sought to pursue the thing she felt she "must do," the "should do" showed up with loud criticism in her mom's voice.

For my client, once we identified that message and voice, we walked through the process of taking authority over that narrative and removed the barrier it was creating in her life. We used her voice to replace the lie. She took ownership of her story and made the necessary corrections.

We started with this one statement . . .

The lie I believed was _____.

The tears started. I was crying with her. Bearing witness to transformation is stunningly beautiful.

The second statement . . .

The truth is _____.

This was the hard part. She had to acknowledge how that message or narrative took a place of ownership in her life when it had no authority to do so. She had to identify the truth and replace the lie.

The third statement . . .

I forgive myself for _____.

This part felt healing and liberating. It was the place where she could honor herself and treat herself with respect. Courage is cultivated in this process.

The fourth and final statement . . .

As a result of this truth, I will _____.

This was the moment of clarity and the beginning of a game plan for confidence moving forward.

Now it's your turn. Use the exercise below Confronting Lies and Uncovering Truth to complete these prompts for yourself.

Exercise #2: Confronting Lies and Uncovering Truth

LIE AND TRUTH #1

Walk through the process of taking authority over the narratives that are barriers and keep you stuck. Remove them by replacing the lie with truth and writing the narrative.

The first step:
The lie I believed was . . .

The second step:
The truth is . . .

This was the hard part. Acknowledge how that message or narrative took a place of ownership in your life when it had no authority to do so. This is where you identify the truth and replace the lie.

The third step:
I forgive myself for . . .

This part is healing and liberating. It is the place where you can honor yourself and treat yourself with respectability and compassion. Courage, clarity, and confidence are collectively cultivated in this step.

The fourth step and final statement:
As a result of this truth, I will . . .

LIE AND TRUTH #2

Walk through the process of taking authority over the narratives that are barriers and keep you stuck. Remove them by replacing the lie with truth and writing the narrative.

The first step:
The lie I believed was . . .

The second step:
The truth is . . .

This was the hard part. Acknowledge how that message or narrative took a place of ownership in your life when it had no authority to do so. This is where you identify the truth and replace the lie.

The third step:
I forgive myself for . . .

This part is healing and liberating. It is the place where you can honor yourself and treat yourself with respectability and compassion. Courage, clarity, and confidence are collectively cultivated in this step.

The fourth step and final statement:
As a result of this truth, I will . . .

LIE AND TRUTH #3

Walk through the process of taking authority over the narratives that are barriers and keep you stuck. Remove them by replacing the lie with truth and writing the narrative.

The first step:
The lie I believed was . . .

The second step:
The truth is . . .

This was the hard part. Acknowledge how that message or narrative took a place of ownership in your life when it had no authority to do so. This is where you identify the truth and replace the lie.

The third step:
I forgive myself for . . .

This part is healing and liberating. It is the place where you can honor yourself and treat yourself with respectability and compassion. Courage, clarity, and confidence are collectively cultivated in this step.

The fourth step and final statement:
As a result of this truth, I will . . .

Systemic Narratives

Identify the narratives you've been told and believed about being successful as a woman. And those narratives are often negative, in particular for women, because of all the external and cultural messages about women, particularly career women. Some of those narratives include:

- Career women don't or can't prioritize their families.
- Career women don't prioritize their personal lives.
- Career women have the hardest time finding a partner and getting married.
- Career women tend to be more domineering or aggressive or too outspoken.

All of these external messages negatively impact our mindset. And that causes us to struggle. It causes us to see ourselves as not valuable, as unworthy. It causes us to struggle to see ourselves in a healthy way.

When there are cultural norms that exist in society, doubled down with the patriarchy and the monochromatic leadership teams within organizations, it's no wonder that it is difficult, incredibly difficult, for women to see themselves in the light of a positive narrative – without spending time doing the reflection and the necessary work to identify where those negative narratives come from, and to uproot the lies that are contained in the negative narratives. Now it's your turn to do the necessary heart work. Walk through your story and reclaim your voice and the grab hold to the truth.

Want to share your thoughts with me?

 Join the conversation and download worksheets from this chapter over on the Courage, Clarity, and Confidence website: www.courage clarityconfidence.com.

10

Decide to Embody the Strongest, Boldest, Most Courageous Version of Yourself

As WOMEN, WE pour so much of ourselves into everything we do – and rightfully so. We tend to be nurturers by nature, and our desire to cultivate something, leaving it better than when we found it, appears to be innate for a large majority. We often bring this perspective and approach to our careers, but frequently without a strategy. We make the mistake thinking that what we pour into our careers we will get back out, but I'm sure you've learned at this point in your career that this just isn't true. Once you come to this realization and become aware of the price of the sacrifice, you'll be ready to do something about it. The unfortunate reality is that in this capitalistic society, what you give will continuously get taken and leveraged for an agenda that rarely, if ever, involves you and your best interest.

Living our lives as a sacrifice, as we women are taught to do by society and culture, disconnects us from our own feelings, needs, and desires. That disconnect is powerful and can be evidenced in our careers. We settle. Far too often, we accept a no that should be a yes. We hustle even harder, to no avail. We exhaust ourselves. We carry the weight of bias, gender inequality, sexism, racism, and harassment.

All. The. Things.

For example:

- How long have you been waiting for a promotion?
- How long have you been overqualified for that job you've been seeking?
- How long have you put up with that toxic culture at the office?

Through the patriarchal, cultural, and economic systems, we are the target.

We go through a cycle, often initiated by an encounter at work that seems off. An overt or covert disparaging comment, microaggression, or insert your specific experience here: _____. We ruminate over it, we hold it in silence for fear we did something wrong. We talk about it in theory with friends. We silently dissect it. We poke holes in our experience. All the while our intuition, eyes, and ears are sure of our interpretation. We come into the awareness that the encounter we had was absolutely unacceptable. We wonder what to do. It doesn't seem "big enough" to take to human resources, but it's "big enough" to not let it go.

You either speak up or you learn to function in silent acceptance. Sometimes you start to speak out, but then you begin to experience repercussions and you start to worry about your reputation, the security of your job, and your future career, and so you retreat. You think, "How can this be?" Doubt creeps in and you ask yourself, "Is it really this bad? Maybe it's me. Did I do something to deserve this?"

Yes, it is that bad. No, you did absolutely nothing to deserve it.

One of the common misconceptions and mistakes we make when we find ourselves stuck in fear and unsure of what to do is to believe that we have limited options or no options at all. Either from our own short-sightedness, limited examples or exposure, or what we are made to believe by those who refuse to validate our experience. It is most commonly the latter.

So what do you do? Tap into resilience, knowledge, and strategy to connect with the strongest, boldest, most courageous version of yourself.

Don't Abandon Your Truth

Truth is a requirement of clarity.

Truth always leads to transformation. Unfortunately, we have a misconception that transformation is comfortable. Similar to the notion that healing is not painful. Both are false.

What I find to be worth the pain is who we become and the laser-focused clarity we have at our disposal once we do the work. The truth of who we are remains, after the stripping away of our old habits and beliefs.

But let's not ignore the systems in place that have sought to keep you from sharing your truth: Women across the globe have to deal with the fear that we won't be believed, that we are overreacting, or that we are doing it for attention – or worse, aggressive – by speaking our truth. There is so much to unpack there, right?

The reality is that seeking to silence, contain, or dismiss our truth is seeking to silence, contain, or dismiss our own voice. And when we become unfamiliar with the sound of our own voice, we become disconnected from ourselves. That opens the doorway for imposter syndrome, self-criticism, and listening to the voices of our loudest accusers, instead of our own.

Connecting with Strength, Boldness, and Courage

Let's channel and connect to your strongest, boldest, most courageous self by visualizing her now. Take a moment and imagine the strongest, boldest, most courageous version of yourself. What would your career look like, if you could choose? What would your life look like?

Picture that version of yourself clearly and consider the following questions. No judging, no filtering, or discarding as you go – just write.

- Who is this version of yourself? What does their life look like?

- What is this version of yourself doing in the day-to-day? Get specific!

- What does it feel like?

- What are you able to do, as this version of yourself, that you couldn't do before?

- Who benefits from this version of you? Whose lives are you impacting?

Taking Action All Begins with Your Best Yes

The Best Yes by Lisa TerKeurst is one of my favorite books.[1] It's a lesson in intentional decision-making and how to say no. A challenge that so many of us have as women is overcoming the tendency to say yes when we really mean an emphatic no. The book is written to help you know how to clarify what's most important to you so that you reserve your yes for what is most important and aligned to you. I had the privilege of reading this book with a small group of phenomenal women in a biweekly book and dinner club. Every other week we talk about the challenges we have faced as women in our careers, our personal life, as well as in dating and relationships.

We discussed why it's so hard to say no in order to give your best yes, and to make ourselves a priority across a variety of experiences we face as women. The common denominator among the six of us was valuing ourselves and trusting that every single no led to the right yes.

Giving your best no means that you're giving your best *yes* to something else. And if you're like most women, you often struggle with saying no and it costs you – a lot – mentally, emotionally, physically. What may seem like a small yes here and there adds up quickly. It gets expensive – giving of our time, energy, resources – and we are the ones left depleted. But there is wisdom in your no that allows you to live your life with more clarity and confidence, but it does take courage.

The courage to say no is the result of knowing yourself intimately, accepting who you are, and honoring who you are by setting and keeping boundaries. As you learn to you value yourself, the process teaches you to value others. As you learn to value yourself and others, you come to understand that saying no is not a burden, but a gift. When we honor our boundaries with a no, it's an invitation to move in alignment with your strongest, boldest, and most courageous self.

Want to share your thoughts with me?

 Join the conversation and download worksheets from this chapter over on the Courage, Clarity, and Confidence website: www.courage clarityconfidence.com.

11

Putting the Pieces Together

IN THE PREVIOUS chapters, I've asked you to get reacquainted with yourself. To intentionally reflect, consider, evaluate, and explore. To go beyond the surface and inquisitively seek out understanding, meaning, and interconnections of your own experiences in your career and life experiences. My goal was to help you see yourself clearly. To recognize who you are, just as you are. And to know how much power you have in your own life and career. To know you are enough. Another degree or certification, while worthwhile, will not change that you are qualified NOW to pursue and achieve your career goals.

If you're like me, navigating each part of the ASCEND practice, before it became a framework, was the first time I really connected with myself from a big-picture perspective, recognized the relationship between the dots in my life and career, and understood the interdependence between my personal and professional life. Up until that point I had always viewed them as separate. I was taught to believe that my professional life gave pathway to my personal life, not the other way around.

Now I absolutely believe that the personal is the pathway to the professional. Identifying, understanding, and coming into alignment with your strengths, values, experience, story, and vision is a power move that gives you the boldness to do anything in your career.

Doing the work contained within each step of the ASCEND practice can be intense, as I am sure you've noticed, but also incredibly transformative. It's a boot camp for you and your career. ASCEND is a wake-up call and a catalyst for change. It requires a lot of introspection, honesty, and compassion with yourself. I mentioned during the introduction of the ASCEND practice that it is in fact a practice. It's not a one-time deal. As you continue to evolve and grow, I'm sure you'll find yourself revisiting some if not all of the steps of the ASCEND practice. I know I revisit elements of the practice often. When I feel stuck, unsure, or can sense that change is on the horizon, I quickly revisit my values and strengths. I grab a journal and pen to explore the questions throughout the practice that help me see the forest and not just the trees.

Before my own initial journey through this practice I had done everything everyone else told me to do and what I thought I *should* do to be successful. As you know, I ended up disappointed and unfulfilled. I had nothing to lose when I decided to go down the rabbit hole of self-exploration, digging into books, assessments, and the like to figure out what was wrong, missing, and needed to be addressed and resolved. I surmised that exploring myself couldn't possibly be worse than sitting with the uncertainty, frustration, and anxiety I was already encountering on my couch night after night.

I realized in those moments that the only person that could give me clear and accurate direction in my career was me. The only person who could make me happy was me. The only way I would be fulfilled in life was if I understood what I needed to be fulfilled. This wasn't about anyone else but me. The dissatisfaction I was experiencing in my career was in large part due to me not understanding and valuing my worth, strengths, values, skills, and experiences. But once understood, I accepted my worth, strengths, values, skills, and experiences. I validated myself. Instead of seeking something externally, I learned to search internally. Success wasn't outside in anymore – it was inside out. I stepped into clarity with a self-confidence I had never experienced before. When you find yourself in that place of awareness, you'll start to notice that you have the courage to rewrite the rules of engagement for how you show up in your life and at work. Moving in confidence with ease and flow. I hope that, as a result, you'll become obsessed with protecting, developing, and nurturing yourself no matter the sacrifice. I also hope you'll realize that those around you, your loved ones, and the rest of the world need more of this version of you.

You Are Your Own Security

The one thing that is certain in this life is that you are your own security. It's not your job or anything else. It's you. When I first learned that principle for myself it was freeing, healing. I felt the heavy weight of fear drop off of me. Since the start of my career, I thought that my security would only come from my ability to "perform" perfectly. I believed that the type of job I had and keeping that job – regardless of the sacrifice – equaled security. Each step of the ASCEND practice revealed to me that luck, coincidence, and perfectionism were not responsible for the achievements and milestones in my career. Instead, it was every decision I made to show up for myself, stand up for myself, come into agreement with my truest self, and move in alignment with the highest version of myself. Your security can be found when you do the same.

Your ability to navigate this mindset shift, that you are your own security, is the catalyst that will change everything as you redefine and pursue your definition of success. Confidence is about establishing security within your identity, your story, and your voice. It takes courage and clarity to get to confidence.

Now that you have navigated through the steps of the ASCEND practice, I have some reflection questions for you that can help you put all the pieces together and inspire you to action to make your vision and voice the priority they should be in your career.

Consider these questions now; at the end of this chapter, you'll have space to tackle them and capture your answers.

- What emotions or feelings did you experience throughout the process?
- What themes, emotions, or feelings do you notice as you read through your responses?
- What were you surprised by, if anything?
- What can you do with what you have learned about yourself through the ASCEND practice?
- What do you want to do with what you have learned about yourself through the ASCEND practice? What is within your locus of control?
- What is one thing, big or small, that you want to commit to as a result of walking through the ASCEND practice?
- How can you implement this one step consistently? When will you begin?

Putting the Pieces Together

Putting all of the pieces together from the ASCEND practice brings clarity. Once you have clarity, you become aware of direction. Identifying your direction gives you a plan for execution.

With those common themes and your core values in mind, craft a personal mission statement for yourself in your future career. Some questions to help you: Who am I? What are my beliefs? What are the core values that guide my life? What is necessary for me to live my best life? How can I and will I impact others?

Example: *I am a catalyst for social justice. I fundamentally believe in the good of the human spirit. My core values are fairness, equality, service to others, and love. As a result of self-care and gratitude, I will show up each day authentically and commit to the advancement of social justice reform initiatives for all. My key skills and experience offer a comprehensive background in nonprofit fundraising, strategic planning, community enablement, and corporate partnerships.*

What could your mission be? Brainstorm in the following blank space. Utilize all of your learnings from the ASCEND practice.

What is your draft mission statement?

How does your mission statement align with where you are now in your career? How is it misaligned?

What can you do to move closer to aligning with your mission?

The Domino Effect

There's a concept I love known as "the domino effect," which is discussed in Gary Keller and Jay Papasan's book *The One Thing*.[1] Keller talks about how critical the domino effect is in creating consistent, repeatable success. How one thing can cause a ripple effect and impact every other area in your life.

A quick overview of the domino effect is:

> If you push the first domino, it will knock over the second one in line, and so on – this phenomenon is called the domino effect. In 1983, a physicist Lorne Whitehead discovered that not only can a domino topple other dominoes – it can topple a domino that is 50% larger.
>
> In other words, the domino effect has a potential of geometrical progression. The term "domino effect" is also used metaphorically, representing a succession of events caused by one single event. In this case, "domino" is a small amount of energy that can cause a chain reaction.
>
> Similarly, if we choose just one thing – one main thing – this will be our first domino. Success is sequential: you do the right

thing, then one more, and more, until they accumulate – in geo-
metrical progression. This doesn't happen overnight – you need
to do one thing at a time, but on a regular basis.[2]

Consider Part II of this book your domino set to success.
Based on what you've read in chapters 4 through 10, considering each step of the ASCEND practice, what is the one domino
or piece of the ASCEND practice that you need to "knock
down" or really lean into first that will then cause a ripple effect,
allowing everything else in your day, week, and ultimately your
life to come into alignment? *Jot down your answer in the following
space.*

Constructing Your Career Arc

Once again, let's look at each piece of the ASCEND practice:

- Acknowledging what is no longer working
- Studying your strengths
- Connecting with your values
- Exploring your professional experiences
- Narrating your story
- Deciding to embody the strongest, boldest, most coura-
  geous version of yourself

These practices all work together to create and lead you on
the pathway to your career arc. An arc is an apex, a peak, the
highest place between two points. Where your career ends doesn't
have to do with where you start; it has everything to do with
what happens in what I call the messy middle.

Our careers are never a linear progression. I haven't met a
single person whose career was a straight line of ascension to

success and fulfillment. Career pathways are messy. Our evolution into who we are becoming is messy too. But I like to think of the ASCEND practice as a guide to help us navigate and make sense of the messy parts of our career journey and ascend to the highest peak we're capable of in our careers.

Each part of the ASCEND practice invites you to get and stay connected with who you are. Keeping yourself in a state of being versus haphazardly doing. The practice gives focus, gets you in the habit of taking action no matter how small to keep you from staying stuck, and empowers you to trust yourself, building confidence to take the necessary steps to excel and accelerate in your career.

Understanding the Practice of ASCEND

Reflection needs honesty.
Honesty requires space.
Physical and mental space.
Consistent space.

Such space is incredibly hard to find at times. But creating the space, not "finding" it, is necessary – that's not even up for negotiation or debate. It can look like 30 minutes, then an hour, then more. It can start once a week, but must move to a consistent, regular cadence. It has to be just as important as taking a shower, eating, and sleeping – the basics.

Your schedule will ALWAYS tell you that "you don't have time." Make your schedule a liar and create the time. And quite frankly, the reason we don't create the time is because we do not want to or believe that we have the capacity to deal with what is there if we make the time to honor ourselves.

Let's also acknowledge the fact that oftentimes we don't believe we truly deserve to be treated with respect given the number of items that are unchecked on our "to-do lists," or the berating narrative that we have to earn time to rest, relax, and reflect. It's a vicious cycle. You are not alone in dealing with this.

There are no prerequisites for rest and reflection. None. Zero. Rest is not something you earn. Anyone who suggests otherwise has no real consideration for your well-being, and that's the cold, hard truth.

If we are going to be "successful," then we have to truly understand who and what we are working with – our beautiful self and everything that comes along with her. One of the first steps you can take in the process of reconnecting with yourself is a regular journaling practice.

As you reflect, you will feel a full range of feelings and emotions. Keep in mind that emotions are objective and feelings are subjective. There are six basic emotions we experience as humans: fear, anger, joy, sadness, disgust, and surprise. We can experience millions of feelings. With that being said, let's start here:

What emotions or feelings did you experience throughout the process?

What themes, emotions, or feelings do you notice as you read through your responses?

What were you surprised by, if anything?

What can you do with what you have learned about yourself through the ASCEND practice?

What do you want to do with what you have learned about yourself through the ASCEND practice? What is within your locus of control?

What is one thing, big or small, that you want to commit to as a result of walking through the ASCEND practice?

How can you implement this one step consistently? When will you begin?

As you consider each of the next set of questions and put pen to paper, I want to encourage you to let curiosity be your guide. This invitation to reflect isn't a place where you're going to be critical of yourself. This is not something where you're going to be judgmental.

Keep in the forefront of your mind that I've invited you into a place of awareness and acknowledgment. Not a berating bash or a pity party. The only goal here is to be courageously honest.

What are you aware of that you were not aware of before?

What do you need to admit to yourself now that you've come into awareness?

What do you need to acknowledge that may have never been truly acknowledged before?

Continuing the Practice of Reflection and Connection

You will need a regular, ongoing practice to facilitate reconnection with yourself and ensure that you are moving in alignment as you curate success in your life.

As you cultivate your practice, the transformation that you experience will shift your mindset from not making yourself a priority to finding that you cannot *not* take the time away to reflect, explore, and listen. It will become a necessary part of your day.

As you spend time getting reacquainted with your voice, here are some questions to help you reconnect with your truest self on a daily or weekly basis:

- What do I want more of?
- What do I want less of?
- What am I trying to control? Why?
- What do I need to release?
- What am I taking responsibility for that is not mine?
- How have I been neglecting myself?

You'll be able to put pen to paper to answer these questions at the end of the chapter. As you spend time with these questions, it is important to keep in mind that the goal is to listen. Not to criticize or judge yourself. You are collecting information and learning more about where you are now so that you can chart a path to the next best version of yourself.

As you begin to communicate with yourself regularly and learn your authentic voice, it may be hard to receive what you are hearing and learning about yourself. But remember what we talked about earlier? Healing and transformation, at first, can be painful, but it is a normal part of the process – and so worth it.

For creatives like myself, sitting still in a quiet room may not be the best way to reconnect with yourself and hear your own voice. You may crave a more creative outlet or a variety of methods of expression to help you on the path back to you. Do things that spark your creativity.

It can be simple things like taking a different route to work and making a note of all that you are grateful for that day. It can be getting out in nature without any distractions and observing how the ecosystem of nature operates. It can also be artistic expression through song, dance, painting, or poetry. It can even be taking on the challenge of learning something new to adopt the mindset that it's okay not to be perfect and "messing up" can be a means of growing and evolving into the next best version of yourself.

Last, but not least, one of my favorites is returning to an old hobby or starting something new. For me, nothing beats the smell of a new book, a fresh pack of pens or markers, and a new journal. I adore reading in bed early in the morning or late at night. I enjoy coming into the awareness that I have time and I am in charge of how I want to spend that time.

Questions for Integrating Reflection in Your Everyday Life

As you spend time getting reacquainted with yourself so you can operate with clarity, here are some questions to help you reconnect with your truest self on a daily or weekly basis:

What do I need today?

How will I honor myself today?

What were my wins today?

What were my learning opportunities?

What am I grateful for?

If you're interested in a deeper dive, consider adding one or more of these questions to your journaling practice:

What do I want more of?

What do I want less of?

What am I trying to control? Why?

How can I give myself grace to operate in ease and flow today?

What do I need to release?

What am I taking responsibility for that is not mine?

Want to share your thoughts with me?

Join the conversation and download worksheets from this chapter over on the Courage, Clarity, and Confidence website: www.courage clarityconfidence.com.

PART

III

Confidence

My mission in life is not merely to survive, but to thrive; and to do so with some passion, some compassion, some humor, and some style.
—Maya Angelou

BEING CONFIDENT IS one of those things that is hard-fought, and extremely powerful once reached. It is an ongoing journey throughout life, but each level of confidence we move through brings us closer and closer to our most authentic selves, empowering us to step into abundance and self-actualization.

In times of uncertainty, we often become desperate for understanding and direction and our confidence dissipates, absolutely nowhere to be found. But the one thing about confidence is that you cannot demand it. It will become elusive if you do, and show up as arrogance and inauthenticity.

Confidence is conviction in action. It is the ability to be certain of your resilience in any circumstance.

Believe it or not, confidence requires stillness as its birthplace. Stillness can remove fear as the driver. In that stillness, there is an invitation to do less, not more, which can feel counterintuitive to the "flight or fight" response that a lack of confidence often incites.

Doing less does not mean doing nothing; however, it does mean doing things that are intentional and productive to help activate and cultivate confidence. When taking an intentional decision to operate in stillness, to do less by focusing on what is most important, taking the time to assess the circumstance before you, you should focus on what it is that qualifies and has prepared you for this moment. It will allow you to make your next best move.

The irony of confidence is that when you begin to initially seek it, it takes time when it feels like time is the very last thing that you have to dedicate toward making a decision.

In this part of the book, that's what I'm going to invite you to do: become still. I know that's the last thing you want to do in a world that's full of chaos and is demanding something from you almost every minute. Being still will help you to be purposeful in your next steps and allow reflection and rest to become your shamans, revealing the answers you need to move forward in your career.

I was recently working with a coaching client. At the top of our call, I asked, as I always do, "What do you want to leave our coaching call with today? She replied, "I want to have more confidence at work." Our session was 45 minutes long. No big deal right?

I simply asked, "Where do you want to start?"

She replied with an overview of the challenges and nuances she was facing at work that were making her feel less sure of herself and her skillset. The difficulties involved a lot of change, tight timelines, new experiences, and high expectations of herself. She was surprised to hear herself say out loud all that was on her plate.

I leaned into curiosity and asked one simple, but BIG question, "What do you need right now?"

She paused. It was a long pause with a deep sigh. Her response, "I need a break, but I can't take one right now." She shut down her needs before we could even explore exactly what her needs were and what it meant to take a break.

Naturally, I asked, "Even though you cannot take one right now, what does a break look like for you?" She described what we would typically refer to as a vacation. While describing her vacation, she was careful to call out that it wasn't rest she needed, but space to be active. To be creative. She needed recreation or what I call *re-creation*. Time to allow our minds, hearts, and body to rest and re-create.

First, why is it so rare that we ask ourselves, "What do you need right now?" Second, in the rare instance that we ask ourselves that question, why do we struggle to give an honest answer?

I think it has a lot to do with fear. Fear that we will not get what we need even if we name exactly what it is. Fear that we'll appear too much or too simple. All potential evidence pointing to our biggest and most present fear – rejection. Lack of validation for our needs.

When I travel for speaking engagements and have the pleasure of getting to know individuals in the audience one-on-one afterward, one of the questions that I'm most often asked is "How are you so confident?" Honestly, I struggled to answer this question for years. I never felt like I had a realistic answer. The truth is, I didn't know how I was so confident. Believe it or not, I never truly felt confident, but what I did feel was convicted; commissioned to do the work that I was and am doing: empowering others.

Every time I took to the stage or platform, I was just seeking to do my best and didn't necessarily feel confident, but knew that my mission was to inspire, help, and serve those who were looking to grow and develop.

What I learned is that *conviction produces confidence*. *Conviction is the result of certainty within*. As we move forward through this part of the book, we'll investigate confidence. It will no longer be elusive or a mystery! We'll explore what it is and how to cultivate it. Then we will discuss the connections between confidence and how it allows us to redefine success on our own terms.

12

Confidence Is Knowing Your Worth

As I LOOK back on different jobs I've held in my career to date, one of the most important lessons I've learned is that you take zero bullshit from anyone. I know, I know, easier said than done, but there comes a point where enough is enough and you have the confidence to accept the consequences that might come as a result of standing up for yourself. Although it might seem like you just want to walk in one day and yell, "I quit!" that rarely ever happens. For me it was a process where rather than continuing to accept the narrative of all of the things I am not, I decided to accept my strengths and realize all of the things I was. While we all have weaknesses, we all also have strengths, and it's important to acknowledge the full spectrum of who you are; that is, giving proper credit to your strengths instead of always highlighting the weaknesses. The challenge for me was to take action while not feeling selfish or that I was disappointing people.

We've all been there. Working hard, getting results, collaborating with colleagues, and anticipating a promotion on the horizon. There's no way you'll be passed over for a promotion this year. The evidence is clear and even your colleagues are excited for you. You've been asked to take on more because of your ability to get things done. The annual moment has come and you know the topic has to be on the agenda. Only to have the meeting and discuss your performance with no peep of a promotion. You decide to ask because surely your boss has forgotten. And when you ask about the promotion, there is surprise as if they were actually unaware. Your boss requests to circle back with you. You accept. And for the next 365 days you receive unclear, vague responses and no actual plan or timeline. Sound familiar?

And when you ask about the promotion the next year, you receive unclear answers and no actual plan or timeline?

I thought so.

After we are passed over for promotion repeatedly, failed to be recognized for our work, start being ignored in meetings, or _____ (insert any one of the thousands of challenges we face in the workplace as women when we advocate for ourselves), we reach a breaking point where something or someone has to change. My experience as a professional and through my work with women as a coach has taught me that you can keep changing *something*, but nothing truly changes until *someone* changes. And that someone is you. But I'm not talking about doubling down on the traditional things we are told to do, by the same leaders who won't promote us. Things like taking on more projects, volunteering for a committee, going to more after-hours events, getting more training, or spending more time on X when it is obvious to every single person around you that you are already doing the work and excelling while doing it. I'm talking about reconsidering the way we define success in our careers, and reevaluating how that definition of success impacts us and what we tolerate as a means to obtain it. Instead of doing more, we need to do less, recognizing that the work we've already done speaks loud and clear. And if our work speaks for us, the absence within our locus of control rests with the confidence that we need not take no for an answer.

It's time to have a mindset shift. Instead of continuing to accept that you're not ready for your desired promotion, what if it's your boss who isn't ready? If they won't honor the value that you bring, determine that you will honor your own experiences, growth, and learning – and move on. Maybe it's time to consider that you've outgrown your boss, the department, or even the company that you're in. I think the goal with some leaders is to keep us so busy that we don't stop to fully evaluate, process, and address that they don't actually know what they are doing while projecting their incompetence on us.

And in the event that we do stop to assess what is truly happening and speak up, we women are labeled as not collaborative, or emotional, or combative, or difficult to work with, even despite evidence that none of those things are actually true. Eventually, we are left with two choices: stay and deal with the drama that turns into trauma, or leave. Far too often, our fear of the risk of leaving – whether to search for a new role or start your own business – wins and we stay in that job until we are completely defeated, or, in today's landscape, included with the next round of layoffs.

When we are faced with those two options, so many different triggers surface and doubt creeps in, limiting our beliefs and mindset. Most of us start our job search at a deficit, which can have long-term impact on our careers and success. It influences which jobs we will apply for, how confident we are in the interview process, and can undermine if and how we negotiate our salaries and compensation packages. In the midst of the challenges at work, there are also often some challenges in our personal lives to add more weight to carry. But the one thing that saved me in my journey – and what will save you too – is learning to trust and listen to your own voice. Reconnecting with the heart, or as Brené tells us, our courage. *You can be trusted.*

After I quit that job, I started my own business. I had no idea what I was really doing or getting myself into, but I trusted myself to figure it out. A good friend reminded me that if things didn't work out with entrepreneurship, I could always get a job somewhere, doing something, to bridge the gap to my next destination. I believed her. She was right.

One of the reasons I started my own business was because I did not ever want to be in a position where I was at the mercy of someone else to dictate to me what I could or could not be, or do. I did not want someone else in control of my livelihood. It was a huge "aha" moment for me. It was at that point in my career that I stopped seeking validation and affirmation of who I was and what I was capable of, and instead decided that I would take control of my career and its progression. I decided to take ownership of my career and ultimately my life.

I learned through that experience, and a host of others, that it will always be my responsibility to know my professional worth and strategically navigate the landscape of work – leveraging all of my professional and personal experience, and always looking for my options. We are never without a choice, even though it may seem like there aren't any alternatives. Courage will always help you find your options.

And the irony of it all, the full circle moment that prompted that leap of faith back in February 2014 was predicated on a lack of professional development and not getting a promotion. Now it's my full-time job to work with women to help them secure their promotions and help them realize they are already ready for what they are seeking. The sheer fact that you are seeking and desire whatever "it" is indicates that you already have everything you need for this next step in your journey and career. See how all things come together for your greatest and highest good?

After a few iterations and evolutions of my own story and business, it is a privilege to help women tap into their courage, gain clarity, and access their confidence to pursue a fulfilling career without sacrificing their values, personal life, or paycheck. Yes. Ma'am. (And yes, I clapped after every period. You read that correctly!)

How Do I Become More Confident?

I'm often asked about my confidence. Questions are different variations of "How are you so confident?" The translation or question behind that question is "How can I be just as confident as you are?" I often struggled when asked this question for two reasons: first, empathy for the woman who doesn't know how to be confident; the second, I don't have an answer because I'm not as confident as you think I am.

True story. Full stop. I've been on hundreds of stages at this point in my life. I even had a two-year speaking tour as a brand ambassador for a paper company. I knew my one-hour-long talk backwards and forwards. Slide deck images were seared into my memory from meticulously creating each one. Yet, I still found myself in bathroom stalls sweaty, nauseous, and prayerful.

My prayer each time was short and succinct: "God you've called me to this place for such a time as this. I don't have what these people need, but you do. Give me the words to speak. Use my gifts, talents, and abilities to help them on their journey. Amen." I would take a series of deep breaths, tighten and release each muscle in my arms and legs to help me minimize the nervous shakes, and then go out on stage. I always requested a handheld microphone (despite all the other cool options) because I would grip the hell out of that microphone to hide how bad my hands would shake sometimes. In the event there was not a handheld microphone available or there were technical difficulties with it, I had a fancy presentation clicker in my bag ready to go. It only took one time for me to experience not having a handheld mic during a presentation for me to order one of the fanciest presentation clickers on the market and spare no expense.

What I learned over the years, after being repeatedly asked that question and stumbling through it, all came to a head during a coaching call with a client. She too was asking how to become more confident. I paused, took a deep breath, and a light bulb went off inside my head.

As a coach, our job is to help our clients unlock the answers they are seeking. I knew it wasn't my job to answer or even advise her. I knew that I needed to ask her a question that would culti-vate awareness.

My question rolled off my tongue with ease, but I felt the depth of the question as I asked, "What convicts you?" In other words, what do you profoundly and unequivocally believe?

We both took a deep breath at the same time. Then there was silence.

She seemed a bit surprised by my question. Truthfully, I was too. I decided to elaborate on the "aha" moment I was having. I'll share with you what I shared with her. It is what I foundationally believe about confidence:

"Conviction creates confidence."

Conviction connects you to your values, purpose, and pas-sion. Until you find and define what convicts you, confidence doesn't show up. Confidence is a powerful attraction energy that draws people and opportunities to you. But that power source doesn't show up and work if it's not connected to your core.

I realized that my ability to get on stage after stage after stage, and be as confident as I was, came from my convictions. I was certain that all of my life experiences prepared me for every stage in front of me. I was certain that I wanted to and could help peo-ple have a career that was aligned with their skills, strengths, and values and be compensated well for it. That their career did not have to consume their entire life and their health. That they could have purpose in their work and be appreciated for their contributions. That work did not have to be their life, but that work could be a component of their life. I am fired up now, just as I was back then!

All that to say, here is the formula for confidence:

Conviction is the birthplace of confidence.

What came up for you when you read that statement? Capture what came up for you as you read that formula in the space below or in your journal.

Confidence is feminine and masculine, but there is a misconception that confidence is a masculine trait. I cannot count the number of times I heard the quest to be more confident described by characteristics that are masculine. As women, we are taught "how to be successful" by utilizing masculine traits as a means to succeed.

Secondarily, confidence often feels so elusive because we think it is outside ourselves, or that we have to become something else. The secret to confidence is to recognize and understand who you are.

When we don't know, appreciate, or value all that we bring to the table, we seek to emulate or mirror those around us who have what we desire – or at least that's what we see from our vantage point. Oftentimes in business, this means taking on more masculine characteristics and behaviors to advance in our careers. And for a period of time, we find ourselves leaning too far into the hypermasculine traits and neglecting the incredible power of the feminine. Far too often, we fight the power of the feminine every day because we are taught to perceive it as a weakness instead of incredible power.

A lot of women feel like they should be more masculine to get what they want, but the last thing we need is more masculine energy in companies. We need to be feminine and show up as ourselves – as women. We've been taught that the masculine is what creates success, but it's not true.

One thing I have noticed from my clients and clients of other coaches is a steady decline in the desire to advance into senior leadership. Many women are realizing that they would rather become an individual contributor who has influence and impact rather than manage others and deal with the politics at the top, not to mention the time constraints and constant demand to give more of yourself to work, which exacerbates the imbalance between work and life. I think that operating for too long outside ourselves and the feminine power we possess creates stress, misalignment, and burnout. Instead of working in harmony with ease and flow, we are working in chaos, driven by leadership that is absent of genuine care, concern for the well-being of others, and valuing human capital as its most significant driver of long-term success and profit.

Want to share your thoughts with me?

 Join the conversation and download worksheets from this chapter over on the Courage, Clarity, and Confidence website: www.courage clarityconfidence.com.

13

Confidence Is Resilience

RESILIENCE IS THE "psychological capacity to adapt to stressful circumstances and to bounce back from adverse events. Resilience is considered a process to build resources toward searching for a better future after potentially traumatic events," Shahram Heshmat writes in *Psychology Today*, noting the eight key elements of resilience:[1]

1. Pursuing a meaningful goal
2. Challenge assumptions
3. Cognitive flexibility
4. Growth through suffering
5. Acting despite fear
6. Emotion regulation
7. The feeling of agency
8. Social support

I don't know a single woman who is NOT resilient. Honestly, when you look up the definition of *resilience*, womankind should be listed FIRST, if you ask me!

If you want to feel, know, and embody confidence, revisit all of your answers throughout each part of the ASCEND practice. Every answer to every question reveals your value, wisdom, skills, strength, and capability. Reflecting on all that you have endured and knowing your potential for the future – to keep showing up everyday – is resilience. You are resilient and you can rely on your resilience to cultivate confidence.

My sister Greta shared something with me years ago and it has stuck with me every hard day since: "*You have survived 100% of your worst days. And even on your worst days, YOU are still better than average. Don't forget that.*" I get emotional every time I say it to myself. My body has a physical reaction where my shoulders drop and the tension eases up. Every time I have a hard moment or day that seems like I can't get through it, I say this affirmation. Every time it shifts my perspective and gives me a boost of confidence that this too shall pass.

We as women face some hard, *rough* days. Things we have yet to vocalize. A lot of those experiences happen at work. But you need to know you are capable and change is always available to you; it just may be a little harder to find sometimes. You have the ability and the courage to do hard things. And one of the best hard things you'll ever do is bet on yourself. You'll win every time.

You're in Control

At a certain point in our careers, we feel that we are no longer in control of our careers. We want to take back control, but we don't know how. Whether it's a terrible manager, the challenges of the job market, an unexpected layoff, the golden carrot, or financial obligations that keep us tied to a job we despise, we feel like the odds are stacked against us. Quite frankly, they are, the majority of the time, but you can take back the control and the agency that rightfully belong to you.

When we are seeking to regain control, what we are really seeking is the confidence to trust that whatever is on the other side of the decision we need to make, we can handle it. When your environment berates you with feedback and commentary that causes you to doubt yourself, you often internalize those experiences and commentary and question yourself.

When women come to me for coaching, particularly those seeking a career transition, I recognize the root of their transition is more often than not about confidence. She's usually burnt out, feeling frustrated about how much she has invested in her current or previous role(s), and has had the final encounter that confirms it's time – for real this time – to make a significant change. Sound familiar?

Like you, she is ready to take a gamble. She has determined that the risk of being perceived as something she is not is far less than the risk of not identifying and fulfilling the purpose in her career and life. Time is of the essence. And for a woman at the executive level, she is occupied with reoccurring thoughts about what her legacy will be. What does all of the time and effort in her career add up to? Was it worth all of the personal sacrifices in the end?

Don't Ignore the Signs

Throughout my career . . . I can remember repeatedly reminding myself at work, and after work, that I should feel satisfied, happy, and appreciative to have a job, a new house, a new car. I started to feel guilty for feeling anything different.

I struggled mentally and emotionally, but maintained the outward appearance of "having it all," especially as a woman of color. As an Enneagram 3: The Achiever, I played by all of the rules, checked all of the boxes, and it felt really good. But I had not "achieved" what I now realize I was looking for: *control* of my time, talent, and the trajectory of my life and career. And with that control I did not know what I wanted until I navigated the ASCEND practice.

In my limited thinking at the time, I thought *control* meant getting a new job. A new challenge. A new environment. A fresh start. Surely, that would bring me a sense of meaning and fulfillment – allowing me to feel in control – right?

That new job, in a lot of ways, appeared to be all of those things. I had new problems to solve, I felt like I had a sense of belonging and necessity, and I had new faces to meet. However, what I realized very quickly was that I was in the same "job" with a little bit more money. I was the same person in a new environment. Changing my job didn't change much and was not the solution I was ultimately seeking. I was still the same person, going home after work every single day, lying on the couch as my mind raced, trying to pinpoint why I was so unhappy.

One cold hard fact that I've learned: You will continue in the same "job" unless you confront the truth about what you're ultimately seeking from a job – and here is the truth bomb – what you are seeking from a job is something that ultimately you can only give to yourself. As career-oriented women, we can become fixated on our jobs, managers and coworkers, and toxic work environments, engaging a cycle of changing jobs to cope with deeper needs that we have to address before we experience fulfillment and the success we desire.

Having agency and ownership of your life starts as an internal transformation and it becomes the catalyst for external transformation. Transformation involves an evolutionary process that leads to transition; in this case, a transition in your career.

Want to share your thoughts with me?

 Join the conversation and download worksheets from this chapter over on the Courage, Clarity, and Confidence website: www.courage clarityconfidence.com.

14

Confidence Is a Habit

As WOMEN, WE often work from a deficit that predisposes our mindset to scarcity instead of abundance. It's rare that we wake up fully rested, energized, prepared, and confident. We might have some of those elements, and we may start our days with all of those intentions, but we typically feel and operate from a place of deficiency instead of abundance. And our mindset around our careers, unfortunately, is no different.

So the million-dollar question becomes, and I get asked this a lot, How do I show up *consistently* from a place of abundance? The second critical question that follows is, How do I show up authentically myself and with confidence?

I would not dare suggest that I have the perfect answer or strategy, but I do want to offer habits that are tried, tested, and true for me and my clients. My clients say these habits were and continue to be the catalyst, a game changer even, regarding how they showed up in any room. These habits continually help them remember their value, come into awareness about how they talk about themselves, and motivate them to execute on their career goals, particularly when navigating a career transition or when seeking a promotion or pursuing work-life integration.

Those habits include:

- Daily affirmations
- Weekly recap
- Regular reflection and journaling (talk about morning pages)
- Engagement with community
- Commit to re-creation
- Move your body

As you review each habit in the following pages, use one or all of them, but remember the goal is to consistently integrate the habit(s) you select into your everyday life, at least five days a week, but you can definitely go for all seven days of the week. These habits will definitely help you manage the Sunday Scaries.

Sunday Scaries

"Feelings of anxiety or dread that happen the day before heading back to work."[1]

In a recent study conducted the job site Monster, up to 76% of Americans self-reported having "really bad" Sunday-night anxiety, compared to just 47% of people around the world.

I don't know about you, but I find that number incredibly high – and can't help but think how much higher that number must be for us as women in particular. I've definitely experienced the Sunday Scaries and it is really tough mentally, emotionally, and physically. In addition to the ASCEND practice, engaging in the following habits truly helped me to manage my anxiety about returning to work on Mondays.

Daily Affirmations

As we mentioned earlier in the book, developing and speaking daily affirmations is a powerful yet easy way to integrate cultivating confidence into your everyday life, so that on days when the to-do list is unbelievably long, you'll be prepared. As you write out your affirmations, consider areas where you want to go, replace a negative narrative with a positive one, and/or consider your future and make statements that are steeped in intention.

I make affirmations a daily habit personally. Over the years some of my own affirmations have included statements like . . .

- My voice has value and it is needed in this room.
- I belong in every room that I find myself in.
- My life is on purpose and for purpose.
- I trust that I can handle anything that comes my way.
- I respect my experiences and they have equipped me for such a time as this.

What could some of your daily affirmations be in this season of life? Feel free to borrow any of mine or do a quick search of affirmations for inspiration.

Weekly Recap

This one is so very simple, but pays dividends in all areas of our career. Do a weekly recap or roundup. This is where you take the time to actually capture tasks completed, accomplishments, lessons learned, connections made, and follow-up items for next week.

I also like to add a self-evaluation or reflection questions too. Capturing lessons learned, revelations, "aha" moments, and the like via pen and paper or digitally. Be sure to capture this information in a way that is easily accessible, organized, and, ideally, searchable.

Make an appointment on your calendar for yourself every single week and KEEP IT. This task isn't just a "nice to do," it's a "must do." I cannot tell you how many times my weekly recaps and up-to-date calendar have been instrumental in performance reviews, meetings, and conversations with work colleagues, especially when coworkers decide to have selective amnesia – we all know those people, don't we!? In full transparency, it's covered my ass as well!

Here are some prompts you can use in your weekly recap or roundup.

- What tasks did I complete this week?
- What tasks are still open and need to be rescheduled?
- What open tasks can be delegated or eliminated all together?
- What were my wins this week?
- What were my learnings this week?
- Whom did I connect with this week?
- What if any follow-up items need to be address as a result of those connections?
- How did I feel this week?
- What did not work for me this week?
- What do I want or need to do differently next week to honor my boundaries?

As you consider this list, what would you add that is specific to your role or industry?

Regular Reflection and Journaling

As you start your journaling practice, start with just writing for a few minutes a day, unfiltered, no holds barred – this is where I am today.

I am a huge fan of Morning Pages, a concept from Julia Cameron, author of the bestselling book *The Artist's Way*. Cameron, who is an astute teacher of reconnecting with our most authentic, creative selves, offers a framework for a daily journaling practice that fosters an ongoing connection with ourselves and a place for our stream of consciousness to flow.

Morning Pages are described as "three pages of longhand, stream of consciousness writing, done first thing in the morning. . . They are about anything and everything that crosses your mind – and they are for your eyes only. Morning Pages provoke, clarify, comfort, cajole, prioritize and synchronize the day at hand. Do not over-think Morning Pages: just put three pages of anything on the page . . . and then do three more pages tomorrow."[2]

As you incorporate a regular journaling practice, utilize some or all of these prompts to help you get to a place of compassion and honor with yourself:

- What will be my affirmation today?
- What truth do I need to remember?
- What do I need right now?
- What is one thing I can reschedule or cancel today to give me more space and capacity?
- Where do I need to extend grace to myself today?

Commit to Re-Creation

As a former workaholic, I used to struggle when I was asked about my hobbies and recreational activities. There was almost always nothing that came to mind. I always felt like an oddball. One day, while working through a new journal with different questions and prompts, I saw the word recreation differently. I saw it as re-creation. It wasn't printed differently, but it definitely jumped off the page in a totally different way.

A message was immediately dropped in my spirit, "You are created by the Creator and you are designed to create." Every creation requires emotional, physical, and mental rest and freedom of expression. Instead of seeing recreation as a time-waster and social conversation piece, I began to view re-creation as a necessary component of wellness and well-being.

Re-creation for me over the years has looked like:

- Arts and crafts
- Travel
- Getting out on the lake
- Time at the beach
- Cooking
- Dancing
- Interior design
- Bullet journaling

Those activities at times were like ministry. Allowing me to use and stimulate my brain in different ways. To have a change in scenery, which served as inspiration and instant way to get unstuck. Re-creation was rest in a new way. Rest is so much more than sleep. Rest in all of its forms is fundamental to having courage, clarity, and confidence.

Quickly brainstorm some ways that you can engage in re-creation here:

Engagement with Community

Moving away from my hometown and having to establish a new local community for the first time made me realize the unparalleled value of having a close, trusted community of friends, advisors, mentors, and even family. Regular connection with my community sharpened me. Gave me laughter. Challenged me. Educated me. Loved me. It is a lifeline and, while not easy to do, you have to find it or reengage with the community you are already a part of in your life.

You may not have the luxury of having an in-person, local community. If that is the case, I encourage you to explore and try out different virtual communities. We have the pandemic to thank for an increase in online platforms and online platform usage. There are several really great online communities for women across different life stages, industries, and social interests.

I encourage you to do your research, don't overthink it, and give one or more of them a try. Who knows, maybe our paths will cross in one of those online community platforms!

Move Your Body

It sounds so very cliché, but it is still so very true. The health benefits of moving your body at any time, but especially in times of increased stress and anxiety, are unparalleled. It is important that we move our bodies, especially as women, considering all of the challenges we have to navigate both inside and outside the office. Let's not forget the impact on our bodies if we choose to birth children.

There is a book called *The Body Keeps the Score: Brain, Mind, and Body in the Healing of Trauma,* by Bessel van der Kolk, that goes into great detail about the impact of trauma on our bodies. It's fascinating to learn about how smart and responsive our bodies are to our needs and what happens when we neglect our bodies.

Moving your body can look like a lot of different things, not just going to the gym. Yoga, dancing, stretching, walking, and lifting weights at home are all things that can contribute to your overall mental, physical, and emotional well-being.

I've offered some recommendations, but would love to hear from you what habits you currently use or are planning to try in order to cultivate and maintain your confidence.

Want to share your thoughts with me?

 Join the conversation and download worksheets from this chapter over on the Courage, Clarity, and Confidence website: www.courage clarityconfidence.com.

15

Redefining Success

What is success?

Who determines it?

Working with my clients, the goal is to help them advance in their career, whether it's a career pivot to a new industry, a job search for a new role, or a promotion within their current career field. Maybe it's taking a step back, prioritizing wellness, implementing work-life integration, or taking a big leap. Whatever the goal, the definition of success always comes into the conversation. When we consider success in our careers, we typically point to socioeconomic status and compensation, specifically salary, as the primary metrics. Women want to be successful and be financially well off, but the traditional definitions of success are proving to be unworthy of the costs to obtain it. Costs like damage to our health, personal relationships, mental health, boundaries, and more. So what we need to do is spend time evaluating our own definition of success and pathways to obtain it. When I work with my clients we explore questions such as:

- What is your personal definition of success?
- Who or what influenced your personal definition of success?
- Whose definition of success are you currently pursuing?
- Are your approach and pursuit of success healthy?

I've held space for you to reflect on and explore those questions below. Use this section jot down your immediate responses to each of those questions.

Defining Success, a Personal Definition

During a coaching session with a client recently, we tackled the question, How do you define "success" in your career?

We both took a deep breath.

I had struggled with this same question a year earlier, so I was well acquainted with how my client might feel. The cracking in her voice let me know the depth of this question moved her to tears.

We discovered that she had a very real fear of success that was impacting her at work and home. She believed that her success would drive a wedge between her and her family. The more successful she was, the more the requests and projects would flood her inbox. Her blueprint for success was what she saw around her, which was to seize every opportunity that came her way. She was subscribed to hustle culture and all that inadvertently comes with it: stress, exhaustion, and a decline in mental health. She wanted to throw all of her success away if it kept her from being the wife, mom, sister, daughter, and aunt she always wanted to be. She also wanted ease, flow, and space.

She had to admit to herself that how she defined success, or more accurately, how success was described for her, wasn't realistic. She had to acknowledge that ease, flow, and space weren't lazy and definitely were not the antithesis to success. She learned this by examining where her definition of success originated.

She ended the session lighter, freer, and with a new mindset. She was clear on her definition and pathway to that success. Laughter and anticipation of next steps filled the last few minutes of our session. She was experiencing flow and ease already.

So when it comes to your definition of success:

- What was presented or demonstrated to you as the first tangible example of success?
- How does that example impact your current definition of success today?
- How would you like to define success now?

Now, I would like for you to consider what it would be like to rewrite the definition of success.

- What would success look like for you, specifically? What is your definition of success?
- What has influenced or informed this revised definition of success?

Once you have answers to those questions, consider the following questions:

- What am I willing to release to obtain it?
- What do I have to embrace to achieve it?
- What am I not willing to sacrifice to become successful?
- What small but intentional actions can I take to make this definition of success a reality?
- What are some longer-term actions that I can plan for?
- Who can help me?

There is space at the end of this chapter to work through your thoughts and consider your answers to each of these questions.

Reimagining Success

Now that you have an increased awareness of who you are, what you are capable of, and the tangibility of evidence to support your incredible value, how can you use that – and all that you've learned through this book – to execute your definition of what it means to be a successful?

As you consider the next steps, I want to share a quick story about a former client of mine who came to me with a lot of disappointment. She came with what I'll refer to as a lot of "*shoulds*" and, to some degree, a sense of regret. This particular client, a doctor, came to me with a lot of predefined external definitions and valuations of what success should be in her life. A narrative of success imposed on her, to which she felt accountable, looked like being a successful doctor, making a certain amount of money working for a prominent medical facility, or eventually having her own practice. Tons, heaping tons, of prestige and ego. Along with a lot of pressure to be what other people thought she should be, do, and have.

There was a culturally predetermined script established for her when it came to being successful. After years of knowing she wasn't being authentic with and to herself, after almost 20 years in her career, she realized that all this time she had neglected her own voice and definition of success. She was struggling to reconcile how she could have been so invested in her career for so many years and still have such a significant gap between where she was and where she wanted to be. She was seeking clarity to make sense of her next steps, but it took courage to be honest with herself once and for all so that she could take confident action.

Even though this awareness was an incredible gift to her, it was a struggle, because she started to feel like she had wasted so much time. So much of her life, so much of her career, spent trying to fulfill someone else's narrative of success for her life. But what she realized is that all that experience was not wasted. It actually gave her the exit strategy she wanted and needed to be able to pursue the second act of her career. Financially, she was able to make some decisions that she otherwise would not have been able to make. She had built enough relationships and cultivated hobbies outside of work that allowed her to have relationships and connections and avenues to pursue the second act of her career.

And that may be you right now, as you're doing this work and asking yourself what is the boldest, strongest, most courageous version of yourself, you may have that moment of awareness where you realize what that version of yourself is and how far away you currently are or have been from that version. And you may start to feel like you've wasted so much time. But I want to encourage you, and realize that at this moment, time is yours as you move forward. You are on time and this moment is happening at this particular season of life for a reason. Don't feel like what you have done in the past has been a complete waste of time, because it is not. I fundamentally believe that nothing is wasted. Instead of looking at what is behind you, focus on how much is still in front of you.

One of my favorite spiritual principles is that God uses all things, not some things, but *all things* to our good. Nothing is wasted. Everything is designed to set you up for purpose and to evolve into the next best version of yourself. I am living proof of that principle. My former client, the doctor, and so many other clients are proof of that too.

My client navigated through the ASCEND practice with our coaching sessions. One of many outcomes from our time together was a career pivot. She turned a hobby and passion project into her career. She realized that part of the pull into the medical field was her love for people and wanting to bring delight to people both young and old. She just needed to change the vehicle in which she delivered that delight. She took over her father's business with her sister. A local dessert parlor with rich community roots and history. What a surprising and beautiful second act. What a great way to recover time with her family and maintain her family's legacy. A reminder that no time is wasted.

So now that you have spent some time reflecting on your personal definition of success with honesty and fierceness, and, I hope, channeled the strongest, boldest, most courageous version of yourself, let's talk about how we move in alignment with your definition of success and achieve it.

Moving in Alignment with Your Definition of Success

The biggest lesson in all of this is to truly understand who you are and what it is that you want, and how you'll move differently, actually achieving your definition of success. It's an opportunity for you to replace limiting beliefs, negative narratives, mistakes, and bad habits with what you now know to be the truth – so you can write and live the next pages and chapters of your story. Getting unstuck, out of the cycle of bad jobs and toxic work cultures, and making decisions with confidence . . . this is your time.

This is how you do the work to move out of those places and to move where you are valued, where you are appreciated, where you get to do work that you enjoy, where you get to be that strongest, boldest, most courageous version of yourself. When we replace the negative narratives, and become well acquainted with who we are, that is when we begin to experience joy and fulfillment. It gives us courage to try new things that we have never tried before. It allows us to play in curiosity and exploration. It allows us to live without fear of repercussions or consequences. And that type of living is what we need more of because that is the transformative living that we crave.

Your Definition of Success in Action: Goal Setting

A few years ago, I attended an enlightening and insightful workshop while attending a conference. I don't even remember the title or overarching focus of the workshop because the concept presented became a total game changer for me, my clients, and the way we approach writing goals.

Here's the concept. There are two types of goals: outcome-based and process-based. The most common way to write goals is outcome-based.

Examples would be:

"I want a new job this year."

"I want to reduce stress in my life."

"I want to_____." Fill in the blank.

"I will_____." Fill in the blank.

With this approach to establishing goals, we're focusing solely on the outcome. The problem with this perspective is that outcome-based goals are primarily outside our locus of control. It does not account for the many factors that impact the achievement of the goal.

Even when applying the SMART (specific, measurable, attainable, relevant, and time-specific) method, most commonly used to deepen our goals, the outcome-based goal still needs to be revisited.

Let's apply the SMART method to the examples mentioned earlier:

> "I want to have a management-level role in product development in the FinTech industry by May."

> "I want to reduce stress this year by taking one to two days of PTO every month to do something relaxing and fun."

While these goals sound strong and have a good approach, the problem is that there needs to be an actual way to measure ongoing progress toward the goal. In addition, the goals do not account for external factors that can impact the achievement of the goal.

Not achieving our outcome-based goals can leave us frustrated, disappointed, and unmotivated. It could potentially cause us to incorrectly assign a label like "failure" to ourselves for not completing the goal, or it could entice us to point the finger of blame at someone or something else. We need to set process-based goals to bring our goals directly within our locus of control, take ownership, and ensure achievement.

Process-based goals are action steps you can control and take consistently to help you reach your desired outcome. It is like developing a healthy habit that sets us up for success to achieve our initial desired goal or even something better.

You want to find a new job this year. In that case, the process-based goal is something like this, "I want to connect with a different person in my network each week to discuss roles in FinTech companies and share my interest in becoming a manager in product development." Setting this goal, as opposed to "I want a new job this year" or even "I want to have a management-level role in product development in the FinTech industry by May," is subtle but different. Once you have your goals, start to build out the specific action steps you'll take each day, week, or month to achieve your process-based goal.

Now comes the real work: Consider this approach to goal setting as you determine actions that will fulfill your definition of success. To help guide you, here are some questions for you to consider:

- What actions can I take to fulfill my definition of success?

- How can I turn those actions into goals?

- How can I turn those goals into process-based goals?

- How will these goals impact my life this year if I achieve them?

■ Are each of these goals directly within my locus of control? If not, what piece of this goal can I take direct ownership of?

■ What process or processes (think habits) do I need to establish on a regular, routine basis – daily, weekly, or monthly – to help me achieve my goals?

■ With whom can I share my goals for accountability and support?

Moving Forward with Your New Definition of Success

What does success mean to YOU?

Get acquainted with what it looks like, but get intimate with what actions it requires daily to achieve your definition and goals. Now develop routines. Allow those routines to become rhythms. Results guaranteed. Success is fixed – meaning, it is inevitable if you implement habits, rhythms, and routines that are aligned with your definitions of success. It is the result of consistency.

At first blush, routines and rhythms sound similar, and they are to a degree. However, my perspective suggests that a rhythm is a tried and tested routine that serves you well enough that you've decided to interweave it into the fabric of your everyday life long-term. Think of it like this: a routine is short-term, and a rhythm is long-term. Whether it's a routine or a rhythm, both start with a micro-decision in your "now." We minimize our "now" because we are too focused on the past or the future. We feel safer in the past or the future because we are too overwhelmed by the pressure and uncertainty of our now. But success is created in the now. There is magic in the moment and in the micro-decisions of rhythms and routines we set every day.

As you focus on and seek to maximize the present, consider the following questions:

- What daily or weekly actions will help you achieve your definition of success?
- What routines can you establish for this month?
- How successful would you become this year if you set healthy routines and rhythms?

Exercise #1: Redefining Success

So when it comes to your definition of success,

- What did you see as your very first tangible example of success?

- How does that demonstration impact your current definition of success today?

- How would you like to define success now?

Now I would like for you to consider what it would be like to rewrite the definition of success.

- What would success look like for you, specifically?

- What has influenced or informed this revised definition of success?

Once you have that definition of your own personal definition of success, consider the following questions:

- What am I willing to release to obtain it?

- What do I have to embrace to achieve it?

- What am I not willing to sacrifice to become successful?

- What small but intentional actions can I take to make this
  definition of success a reality?

■ What are some longer-term actions that I can plan for?

■ Who can help me?

Exercise #2: Goal Setting with Rhythms and Routines

■ What are my process-based goals?

■ Why did I set this/these goal(s)? What is my why?

- How will these goals impact my life this year if I do or do not achieve it?

- Are each of these goals directly within my locus of control? If not, what piece of this goal can I take direct ownership of?

- What process or processes (think habits) do I need to establish on a regular, routine basis – daily, weekly, or monthly – to help me achieve my goals?

- Who can I share my goals with for accountability and support?

Want to share your thoughts with me?

 Join the conversation and download worksheets from this chapter over on the Courage, Clarity, and Confidence website: www.courageclarityconfidence.com.

16

The Future of Women + Work

SOME FINAL THOUGHTS as we consider women and work in the future.

I hate to be the one to say this, but I can be impatient. I am tired of waiting for systemic change; however, I'm simultaneously committed to the long game. I'm a mom, an aunt, a sister, a mentor, and champion for women, clearly. But what do you do in the meantime, as slow but steady progress moves us forward? How do you maintain hope? Sleep at night?

I don't have the answers, but I do hope the principles and exercises in this book are the beginning of massive healing, transformation, and one of the biggest catalysts for change in your career and life. I hope that these exercises have and will continue to implore you to show up fully confident, crystal clear, and courageously ready to join hands with other women to shake up the workforce by no longer playing small, having the audacity to quit or pivot, and creating new pathways for women of the future to follow.

I was recently asked what I think will happen with women and work in the future. There's so much I could hope for and I have a lot of ideas, but it is hard to tell. You can never accurately predict the future. Consider the pandemic and how it literally changed everything so quickly. But if I use what I know and have observed with current patterns and trends post-pandemic, I would make the following assumptions. I wouldn't dare suggest that they are fixed and accurate, but the research and work would bend in the following directions when it comes to women and work.

We will continue to see a rise of women leaving the workforce to start businesses.

The pandemic was a huge shift for the workforce and women were the hardest hit. It's no surprise that women demonstrated incredible resilience turning massive layoffs and mass exits on their heads to start businesses, become freelance professionals, consultants, and independent contractors. The pandemic provided a shared experience of what work-life integration could look like long term without sacrificing the bottom line to the business. It's nearly impossible to let that shift go when it afforded so many of us more time with our families, reduced stress from toxic work cultures, and more flexibility in when, where, and how we work.

There will be an increase in funding for women- and minority-owned businesses from investors, but also, most notably, from the federal government in a big way in an effort to address economic turmoil.

Due to the rise of women entrepreneurs, the single largest growing class of entrepreneurs are women, Black women to be specific. I believe we will continue to see women push back on antiquated workplace policies, toxic workplace cultures, and in-person work requirements that exceed three days a week. They will trade it all for better work-life integration, family, mental and physical health, and economic preservation. No longer will women lose as much ground while out of the traditional workforce. Entrepreneurship and funding will allow them to close, at least to some degree, the earning gap.

I believe the number of women leaving the workforce will continue to swell and that the federal government maybe forced to intervene. The great resignation will continue for women.

We will see an increase in women in political office.

When the Roe v. Wade decision came down, it caused not only a major rift, but a shift. Women on both sides of the aisle were emboldened to speak up and take action. Similarly, the increase in mass shootings in schools met with no swift political change, provoking women yet again. These matters and *so many* others enlarge the gap in trust with currently elected officials. More women will have the courage and confidence to take their values and convictions to the public political stage to enact change.

Mental health concerns will become a public health crisis.

In Ellevest's 2022 financial wellness survey, mental wellness was at the top of the list of priorities for women, with 48% of participants responding, as compared to 35% in 2021.[1] It is the first time that mental wellness has been a higher priority than financial wellness. We've also all seen the rise in ease of accessibility to connect with a therapist through a variety of media, programs, and platforms. For the first time in history, the United States rolled out a universal, free suicide and crisis helpline (988) to acknowledge the prevalence of mental health concerns and the significant gap with resources. When mental health does become a public health crisis, it will cause a shift in the workplace as the government seeks to intervene by strongly encouraging or even mandating specific workplace policies and benefits. I would like to see a tax credit or benefit, such as a write-off, for those who participate in therapy or counseling for mental health and wellness.

Companies will begin to improve policies on workplace culture and benefits with an orientation to caretakers across all

genders if they want to stay viable. There will be federal incentives that will anchor this shift.

The mass exodus of women at work will drive companies to improve workplace policies and benefits that bring caretaker responsibilities to the forefront. We will see a reemergence of remote and hybrid roles again as companies continue to compete for top talent and to survive economic transitions. With workplace cultures and environments top of mind for the US Surgeon General, more pressure will be applied to companies to take action. I foresee incentives from the government, particularly to small to mid-size businesses, that adopt company policies and benefits for caretakers and women in consideration.

Maybe I am unrealistically optimistic and my assumptions are merely hopes for what will happen, but what I know for sure is that the workforce will never be the same post-pandemic, and there will be other systemic crises that force additional requisite changes with the way we work.

Want to share your thoughts with me?

 Join the conversation and download worksheets from this chapter over on the Courage, Clarity, and Confidence website: www.courage clarityconfidence.com.

Acknowledgments

GRETA, GELICIA, AND GENESIS, your sisterhood, and more importantly your friendship, have saved my life. Knowing that we have each other to lean on in times of despair and to celebrate life's milestones has literally meant everything to me. Every laugh, every tear, I count as a blessing. I cannot thank God enough for knitting our biological and spiritual hearts together.

George, you believed in me from the day you met me and have been steadfast in that belief. You've been an anchor for this creative soul. Thank you for celebrating with me and always being my home.

LaBonnae, the color of the cover of this book makes so much sense now. You saw it on bookshelves before I did. I carry your spirit with me. It was a privilege to have your flame strengthen mine. It burns brighter because of you. Our friendship transcends this earthly realm. I'll meet you at Barnes & Noble!

To all of the clients I've worked with throughout my career, thank you for teaching me. Thank you for trusting me to walk alongside you in some of the most vulnerable parts of your journey. Thank you for making me a better coach, friend, and human.

To Ariel, my first book writing coach: In the beginning of this process, you affirmed me when I didn't know if had what it took to actually write a book. You validated my perspective, writing style, and intuition. I appreciate your encouragement and support.

To Susan, learning how to be a coach under your guidance and leadership has been a cherished blessing. I really do count it as an honor to have learned and to continue to learn from you. Your compassion, expertise, and zest to make the world a better place through coaching is an inspiration.

To Ashleigh, one piece of advice you gave me unlocked something on the inside of me and words poured into this book differently. Thank you for always having a beautiful spirit and living out your testimony.

About the Author

Gala Jackson is passionate about helping women stand in the power of their femininity. As a certified and accomplished executive career and leadership development coach, she works with domestic and international women to redefine and take ownership of their success. She empowers women to discover and live in alignment with the strongest, boldest, most courageous version of themselves.

Recognized for her practical coaching strategy, she emboldens women to step into courageous awareness, gain clarity, cultivate confidence, and develop their leadership style through strengths – and values-based coaching. Her expertise has appeared in the *New York Times, Marie Claire, Essence, Huffington Post, Millie* magazine, and other national publications. She's helped thousands of professionals navigate career transitions to find career satisfaction and significance without sacrificing lifestyle or compensation. In addition to her coaching work, Gala partners with organizations to deliver high-impact keynote presentations, workshops, and retreats on career and leadership development topics that impact women.

Gala holds a master's in educational leadership and a bachelor of fine arts in communication. Outside of her mission-focused work, Gala enjoys yoga, journaling, reading, and is a self-proclaimed foodie. She spends quality time on the beach or family farm with her husband and son.

www.galajackson.com

www.linkedin.com/in/galajackson

www.courageclarityconfidence.com

Notes

Part I

1. *Merriam-Webster Dictionary*, https://www.merriam-webster.com/dictionary/courage

Chapter 1

1. Abigail Johnson Hess, October 16, 2019, https://www.cnbc.com/2019/10/16/womens-earnings-drop-after-having-a-childbut-mens-do-not.html
2. The US Surgeon General's Framework for Workplace Mental Health & Well-Being, 2022, pp. 6–7, https://www.hhs.gov/sites/default/files/workplace-mental-health-well-being.pdf
3. Megan Cerullo, October 25, 2022, https://www.cbsnews.com/news/toxic-workplaces-are-bad-for-your-physical-health-surgeon-general/
4. Lean IN and McKinsey & Company, *Women in the Workplace 2022*, p. 5, https://womenintheworkplace.com/
5. Casey Kuhn and Nicole Ellis, October 18, 2022, https://www.pbs.org/newshour/economy/what-is-quiet-firing-and-how-do-you-know-if-its-happening-to-you
6. Katica Roy, September 6, 2022, https://fortune.com/2022/09/06/women-workforce-fed-rates-consider-full-employment-katica-roy/

7. Alexandra York and Marguerite Ward, February 6, 2023, https://www
.businessinsider.com/black-women-leaving-corporate-america-entreprenurship-
startups-2022-12

8. York and Ward, https://www.businessinsider.com/black-women-leaving-
corporate-america-entreprenurship-startups-2022-12; the Department of
Labor table mentioned in the article can be found at: https://www.dol.gov/
agencies/wb/data/lfp/lfp-sex-race-hispanic

Chapter 2

1. Brené Brown, *Integration Idea: Permission Slips*, p. 1, https://brenebrown
.com/wp-content/uploads/2021/09/Integration-Ideas_Permission-Slips_
092221.pdf

Chapter 3

1. Dictionary.com, https://www.dictionary.com/browse/alignment

Part II

1. *Merriam-Webster Dictionary*, https://www.merriam-webster.com/dictionary/
clarity; https://www.merriam-webster.com/dictionary/clear

Chapter 4

1. Robin Clark, December 6, 2021, Instagram, @loverobinclark, https://
www.instagram.com/p/CXKjYjiMw70/

Chapter 6

1. Chris Kolmar, February 6, 2023, https://www.zippia.com/advice/how-
many-applications-does-it-take-to-get-a-job/

2. Gallup, Inc., "Use the CliftonStrengths Assessment to Discover & Develop
Your Greatest Talents," https://www.gallup.com/cliftonstrengths/en/
253676/how-cliftonstrengths-works.aspx#:~:text=It%20only%20takes%
20177%20questions,need%20to%20maximize%20your%20potential

Chapter 7

1. Craig Groeschel, *Chazown: Discover and Pursue God's Purpose for Your Life* (Multnomah, 2010).

Chapter 8

1. Google Dictionary, https://www.google.com/search?q=clarity+definition& oq=clarity+defin&aqs=chrome.0.0i433i512j69i57j0i512l8.2902j1j7& sourceid=chrome&ie=UTF-8
2. Amy Hale, "Can We Change Ourselves Simply by Changing Location?" *Psychology Today* (February 8, 2012), https://www.psychologytoday.com/ us/blog/the-power-places/201202/can-we-change-ourselves-simply-changing-location

Chapter 10

1. Lisa TerKeurst, *The Best Yes* (Nelson Books, 2014).

Chapter 11

1. Gary Keller and Jay Papasan, *The One Thing: The Surprisingly Simple Truth About Extraordinary Results* (Bard Press, 2013).
2. Natalia Rossingol, "The One Thing: Book Summary in 10 Minutes," June 22, 2022, https://www.runn.io/blog/the-one-thing-summary#:~:text= people%20might%20imagine.-,2.,domino%20that%20is%2050%25%20 larger

Chapter 13

1. Shahram Heshmat, "The Eight Key Elements of Resilience," *Psychology Today*, May 11, 2020, https://www.psychologytoday.com/us/blog/science-choice/202005/the-8-key-elements-resilience

Chapter 14

1. Headspace, n.d., "How to Beat the Sunday Scaries," https://www.headspace .com/articles/sunday-anxiety#:~:text=What%20causes%20the%20 Sunday%20Scaries,before%20heading%20back%20to%20work

2. Julia Cameron, 2023, "Morning Pages," https://juliacameronlive.com/basic-tools/morning-pages/

Chapter 16

1. The Ellevest Team, September 22, 2022, https://www.ellevest.com/magazine/disrupt-money/ellevest-financial-wellness-survey-2022

Index

195